SUBCULTURES

THE BASICS

Subcultures: The Basics is an accessible, engaging introduction to youth cultures in a global context. Blending theory and practice, this text examines a range of subcultures such as hip hop, graffiti writing, heavy metal, punk, burlesque, parkour, riot grrrl, straight edge, body modification, and skateboarding. Using case studies from around the world, this text answers the key questions posed by those new to the subject, including:

- What is a subculture?
- How do subcultures emerge, who participates, and why?
- What is the relationship between deviance, resistance, and the "mainstream"?
- How does society react to different subcultures?
- How has global media and virtual networking influenced subcultures?
- What happens when subcultural participants "grow up"?

Tracing the history and development of subcultures to the present day, with further reading and resources throughout, this text is essential reading for all those studying youth culture in the contexts of sociology, cultural studies, media studies, anthropology, and criminology.

Ross Haenfler is Associate Professor of Sociology at the University of Mississippi, USA. He teaches courses on subcultures and social movements, and his research interests revolve around youth cultures, gender, and how people pursue social change in their daily lives.

The Basics

ACTING
Bella Merlin

AMERICAN PHILOSOPHY
Nancy Stanlick

ANCIENT NEAR EAST
Daniel C. Snell

ANTHROPOLOGY
Peter Metcalf

ARCHAEOLOGY (SECOND EDITION)
Clive Gamble

ART HISTORY
Grant Pooke and Diana Newall

ARTIFICIAL INTELLIGENCE
Kevin Warwick

THE BIBLE
John Barton

BIOETHICS
Alastair V. Campbell

BUDDHISM
Cathy Cantwell

THE CITY
Kevin Archer

CONTEMPORARY LITERATURE
Suman Gupta

CRIMINAL LAW
Jonathan Herring

CRIMINOLOGY (SECOND EDITION)
Sandra Walklate

DANCE STUDIES
Jo Butterworth

EASTERN PHILOSOPHY
Victoria S. Harrison

ECONOMICS (SECOND EDITION)
Tony Cleaver

EDUCATION
Kay Wood

EUROPEAN UNION (SECOND EDITION)
Alex Warleigh-Lack

EVOLUTION
Sherrie Lyons

FILM STUDIES (SECOND EDITION)
Amy Villarejo

FINANCE (SECOND EDITION)
Erik Banks

FREE WILL
Meghan Griffith

HUMAN GENETICS
Ricki Lewis

HUMAN GEOGRAPHY
Andrew Jones

INTERNATIONAL RELATIONS
Peter Sutch and Juanita Elias

ISLAM (SECOND EDITION)
Colin Turner

JOURNALISM STUDIES
Martin Conboy

JUDAISM
Jacob Neusner

LANGUAGE (SECOND EDITION)
R.L. Trask

LAW
Gary Slapper and David Kelly

LITERARY THEORY (SECOND EDITION)
Hans Bertens

LOGIC
JC Beall

MANAGEMENT
Morgen Witzel

MARKETING (SECOND EDITION)
Karl Moore and Niketh Pareek

MEDIA STUDIES
Julian McDougall

THE OLYMPICS
Andy Miah and Beatriz Garcia

PHILOSOPHY (FIFTH EDITION)
Nigel Warburton

PHYSICAL GEOGRAPHY
Joseph Holden

POETRY (SECOND EDITION)
Jeffrey Wainwright

POLITICS (FOURTH EDITION)
Stephen Tansey and Nigel Jackson

PUBLIC RELATIONS
Ron Smith

THE QUR'AN
Massimo Campanini

RACE AND ETHNICITY
Peter Kivisto and Paul R. Croll

RELIGION (SECOND EDITION)
Malory Nye

RELIGION AND SCIENCE
Philip Clayton

RESEARCH METHODS
Nicholas Walliman

ROMAN CATHOLICISM
Michael Walsh

SEMIOTICS (SECOND EDITION)
Daniel Chandler

SHAKESPEARE (THIRD EDITION)
Sean McEvoy

SOCIAL WORK
Mark Doel

SOCIOLOGY
Ken Plummer

SPECIAL EDUCATIONAL NEEDS
Janice Wearmouth

TELEVISION STUDIES
Toby Miller

TERRORISM
James Lutz and Brenda Lutz

THEATRE STUDIES (SECOND EDITION)
Robert Leach

WOMEN'S STUDIES
Bonnie Smith

WORLD HISTORY
Peter N. Stearns

SUBCULTURES

THE BASICS

Ross Haenfler

Routledge
Taylor & Francis Group

LONDON AND NEW YORK

First published 2014
by Routledge
2 Park Square, Milton Park, Abingdon, Oxon OX14 4RN

and by Routledge
711 Third Avenue, New York, NY 10017

Routledge is an imprint of the Taylor & Francis Group, an informa business

© 2014 Ross Haenfler

British Library Cataloguing in Publication Data
A catalogue record for this book is available from the British Library

Library of Congress Cataloging in Publication Data
A catalog record for this title has been requested

ISBN: 978-0-415-53031-6 (hbk)
ISBN: 978-0-415-53029-3 (pbk)
ISBN: 978-1-315-88851-4 (ebk)

Typeset in Bembo
by Taylor and Francis Books

Printed and bound in Great Britain by
TJ International Ltd, Padstow, Cornwall

To my daughter, Wren, and all of the adventures we'll have together.

CONTENTS

Preface   x
Acknowledgements   xii

1   What is a subculture?   1

2   How do subcultures emerge and why do people
    participate?   27

3   How do subcultures resist "mainstream"
    society ... and are they successful?   42

4   Who participates in subcultures?   61

5   Who are the "authentic" participants and
    who are the "poseurs"?   82

6   How does society react to subcultures?   101

7   Have subcultures gone virtual? Global?
    Where do subculturists hang out?   118

8   What happens to subculturists as they "grow up"?   139

    Bibliography   156
    Index   176

PREFACE

Scholarly studies of subcultures have a rich history and seem to only be gaining steam, as people who grew up participating in scenes go on to become subcultural scholars. The topic is certainly close to my heart. Not only do I teach, research, and write about subcultures, I grew up in the punk, heavy metal, and straight edge scenes. The more I learn about the vast array of subcultures, the more I appreciate what they teach me about my own life and the larger social worlds in which I live.

I hope that for students new to subcultures this book serves as a gentle but thorough introduction to a very rich and complicated field. As the title promises, you have before you its basic history and essential topics. You will see that I have organized the book in terms of common questions people raise about subcultures: How do they emerge? Why do people participate? How does society react? and so on. Perhaps just as importantly, each chapter includes a variety of citations and suggestions for further study, enabling you, I hope, to more thoroughly pursue the topics most interesting to *you*. Rather than include a glossary, I have bolded important terms and ideas in the text and the index to highlight particularly important concepts.

For scholars of subcultures, my wish is that the book encourages the already fruitful emerging developments in the field, including how space and place shape subcultural experience; how critical race theory and queer studies might better inform our work; a more thorough investigation of globalization; new studies of ageing and subcultural participation across the life course; expanding the concept beyond music and "spectacular" scenes; and continued investigation into subculturists' virtual experiences. Additionally, I hope that academics explore the connections between subcultures and related concepts, including social movements, lifestyles, and lifestyle movements.

Finally, should this book find its way into the hands of subculturists, I hope you find something of your own lives reflected herein. A text cannot hope to fully capture the meanings, emotions, and relationships embedded in subcultural experience, but perhaps you will find new ways of thinking about your life, ways of making the familiar unfamiliar, perhaps even in empowering ways.

ACKNOWLEDGEMENTS

I am grateful to everyone at Routledge who at various times have given input on this project, particularly Sophie Thompson, Rebecca Shillabeer, and Iram Satti. I am thankful for fantastic, supportive colleagues at the University of Mississippi, and for a terrific family who accept my subcultural idiosyncrasies. My wonderful partner, Jennifer Snook, has been exceptionally patient throughout my various projects, looking over chapters and listening as I worked through writing struggles. I am also grateful to you, the reader, for picking up this book. I would love to hear from you.

WHAT IS A SUBCULTURE?

I grew up in the 1980s amid a resurgence of youth subcultures, witnessing firsthand the growing concern for the fate of America's kids. Youth, it seemed, were headed for trouble. Hippies were long gone and disco was on the decline, replaced by hip hop, hardcore, and heavy metal. Whereas hippies and disco freaks raised alarms about drugs and free love, gangsta rap allegedly sparked inner city ultraviolence, prompting kids to abandon school for guns and gang life. Ice-T and NWA gained notoriety for both their explicit sexual references and their flagrant disdain of police. Not to be outdone, heavy metal lured alienated youth into cults and devil worship, while its glam metal counterparts took the sex, drugs, and rock 'n' roll lifestyle to new extremes. Iron Maiden's song "The Number of the Beast" incensed religious leaders, as did gender-bending groups such as Poison and Mötley Crüe, who plastered themselves with makeup and teased their long hair to impossible heights. Meanwhile, Black Flag helped transform punk rock into the even more aggressive hardcore, prompting police to harass the band and shut down shows. Their fans gained such a reputation for violence that some clubs blacklisted them from playing.

Outside the music scene, the fantasy role-playing game Dungeons & Dragons skyrocketed in popularity, players rolling oddly-shaped dice in efforts to slay imaginary goblins, orcs, and other mythical beasts. Parents and religious leaders saw the game not as fun, imaginative play but rather a Satanic recruitment tool that encouraged suicide, murder, and witchcraft. When youth weren't busy joining cults or doing drugs they were wasting time on their skateboards as Tony Hawk's gravity-defying acrobatics on the vertical ramp furthered the sport's popularity. They might even ride those skateboards to the local arcade to waste *more* time (and money) playing video games, although the invention of the Atari 2600 and other gaming consoles meant kids could play Pac-Man and blow up tanks without leaving the comfort of their couches. Graffiti writers and gangs accelerated urban decline while in the UK football hooligans became society's bogeymen, spreading fear throughout the terraces. Nazis infiltrated the punk scene and white power organizations began recruiting skinheads to their cause. Alarmed by the sheer breadth of deviant activity, authorities of various stripes formed task forces, filed lawsuits, convened legislative hearings, preached sermons, expanded surveillance and policing, fought wars against drugs, and locked young people up in record numbers. Subcultures, always suspect, were officially dangerous.

To quell the growing threat, conservative governments pledged law and order even as they cut holes in the social safety net, while a resurgent religious right called for a return to moral values, fending off feminists and gay activists in an ongoing battle to rectify the spiritual lapses of the 60s. This charged atmosphere led to several awkward conversations with my parents. Why did I want to grow my hair long like the guys in Metallica? Was my D&D playing leading to an unhealthy interest in the occult? Just what *were* those punk bands screaming about? And why were there demons and pentagrams on my Slayer records? In the decades since the 80s, the number and variety of subcultures has only increased, meaning, no doubt, that more young people suffer these same uncomfortable conversations.

To outsiders, subcultures can seem alternately strange and silly, mysterious and dangerous, or all of the above. They appear as bizarre little worlds with secret signs, idiosyncratic rituals, fantastical styles, and arcane social codes. Yet popular perceptions of sub-cultures are often incomplete, little more than caricatures based upon half-truths or hysteria. Many subculturists are not so terribly different, leading well-adjusted, productive, and meaningful lives (at least as much as anyone can claim to do so). While certainly not saints, neither are they typically the devils the media portrayed in my youth. These alternating visions demonstrate the need for careful study, to better understand the motivations, beliefs, and practices of subcultural groups – and why so many people find solace in the company of fellow outcasts.

In this chapter, I briefly map the history of subculture studies, beginning with the Chicago School and ending with contemporary work. I will outline the difficulties of defining "subculture" before offering a working definition. Finally, I discuss subcultures' conceptual differences and similarities to other collective behavior such as gangs, social movements, and fandoms.

A BRIEF HISTORY: HOW HAVE SCHOLARS STUDIED SUBCULTURES?

CHICAGO SCHOOL – URBAN DEVIANCE

The University of Chicago housed one of the first sociology departments in the United States, including some of the early pioneers of the field. While few Chicago School scholars used the term "subculture" as we understand it, their insights regarding social problems, crime and deviance, immigration, urban life, and research methodology continue to be relevant to subcultural studies today.

Life in Chicago, and other rapidly growing industrial cities, was far from easy, particularly for the various immigrant groups that worked long hours in the mines, factories, and sweatshops. Author Upton Sinclair described immigrants' experience of dangerous, backbreaking work in a Chicago slaughterhouse in his 1906 novel *The Jungle*, revealing the countless hardships faced by poor families struggling to survive in their new homeland. Such contexts inevitably produced a variety of social problems, including crime and delinquency. Religious leaders, urban planners, and social workers sought to understand such problems for practical reasons: knowledge of communities, including youth subcultures or gangs, would help reformers "fix" social problems and "save" people from leading lives of crime (Cavan 1983). An early advocate for working-class immigrants and a colleague of what later came to be known as the Chicago School, Jane Addams founded Hull House, a community-building and resource center, using studies of the neighborhood to guide her social reforms (Deegan 1988). According to the Chicago School theorists, crime and poverty were the result not of individuals' personal, moral, or psychological failings per se, but rather products of the *social* environment. Deviance was a symptom of social problems, especially the inequality produced by rapid social change (including urbanization), and especially in "transition zones" in which disadvantaged groups are often forced to live (Shaw and McKay 1942). For example, W. I. Thomas and Florian Znaniecki's study of Polish immigrants addressed the "tendency to disorganization of the individual under the conditions involved in a rapid transition from one type of social organization to another" (Thomas and Znaniecki 1918–1920: viii). This insight is central to subcultural studies in that "deviant" behavior – whether stealing a car or piercing one's lip – exists in the context of larger social arrangements. Only by understanding the greater context in which subcultures exist can we more closely grasp subculturists' motivations and experiences.

Early Chicago scholars Robert Park and Ernest W. Burgess (1922) saw cities as organic entities, developing a theory of **human ecology** that compared social life to biological organisms. Much like an organism, social groups are composed of various parts that more or less function together for the stability of the whole. Competition and conflict produce accommodation, whereby people adjust to new conditions and return to "equilibrium" (Park and Burgess 1922: 664). Rapid migration, industrialization, political upheaval, technological innovation, and economic change disrupt that equilibrium and the social control societies provide. In other words, **social disorganization** produces deviance and street crime – city "zones" with high unemployment, poverty, and population turnover produce higher crime rates than more stable areas, regardless of which group of people lives there. So gangs and groups of delinquent boys were products of their environment rather than irredeemable sinners or hopeless criminals with inherent imperfections. For criminologists then, "subculture" was (and sometimes still is) used to describe a delinquent or criminal gang to be stopped or reformed by various authorities.

Other scholars connected with the Chicago School contributed important ideas to subculture studies and refined the ethnographic methods many contemporary scholars employ. Nels Anderson published *The Hobo* (1923), a field study of Chicago's homeless population, building on the tradition of studying the problems of marginalized groups. Observing Chicago gangs, Frederic Thrasher (1927) highlighted the importance of gangs as communities emerging from the ordeals of living in downtown slums, and Paul Cressey (1932) observed taxi-dancers, women who danced with men for money. Later, William Foote Whyte lived for three and a half years in an Italian neighborhood ("Cornerville") in Boston's North End, even learning to speak Italian as he investigated youth gangs, social clubs, criminal organizations, and political machines. He found that seemingly "disorganized" slums actually have a complicated social structure: "Cornerville's problem is not lack of organization but failure of its own social organization to mesh with the structure of the society around it" (Whyte 1955 [1943]: 273). Edward Franklin Frazier wrote the groundbreaking *The Negro Family in the United States* (1939), highlighting how the *social* conditions of slavery and Jim Crow echoed into the future, impacting personal identity, black family forms, and social problems. Significant social changes, including Prohibition, the Great Depression, and eventually World Wars I and II pushed some into petty crime and racketeering.

STRAIN THEORY

The (now) basic idea that social conditions play a role in producing delinquency and crime is still relevant today, although authorities, politicians, and much of the public still rely primarily on individualistic explanations of deviance. In 2005, a series of riots rocked Paris, perpetrated primarily by North African immigrant youth living in poor *banlieues* (low-income suburbs). Rather than vilifying these youth as evil purveyors of random mayhem, a more *social* explanation would look to their marginalized status in French society – for example, high unemployment, police harassment, and racism. Similarly, as US cities experienced deindustrialization and white flight since the 1960s, gangs thrived among inner city youth. Attempting to explain deviance, Robert Merton (1938) suggested that denied *legitimate* access to society's cultural goals (e.g. wealth, status, power) some individuals will inevitably turn to *illegitimate* means of achievement, including crime. The psychological strain imposed by the disconnection between culturally proscribed aspirations and lack of legitimate opportunity provoked deviance and even, at times, rebellion. Albert Cohen followed up on this idea in his enormously influential book *Delinquent Boys* (1955), but saw strain in more social terms, suggesting that deviant subcultures emerged as a reaction against status frustration, or blocked opportunities. If society's goals seemed out of reach, youth turned instead to deviant goals, substituting subcultural achievements for notions of conventional success.

Another wave of American scholars, often inspired by early Chicago sociology, hugely influenced the contemporary study of subcultures. Howard Becker's (1963) **labeling theory** proposed that deviant acts and people are not *inherently* deviant but only become deviant once people label them so. The degree to which authorities deem subculturists strange or their way of life threatening influences the societal response and, subsequently, how subculturists view themselves. Thus deviance is a *social* phenomenon involving an often-unequal contest over the meanings of non-normative behaviors and identities. Similarly, Erving Goffman's (1963) work on social **stigma** – discrediting attributes whereby others judge us as untrustworthy or incompetent – and on **stigma management** – how people attempt to control or manage others' judgments – is enormously helpful in understanding subculturists' relationship to dominant society (see Chapter 6). Subcultures are defined not only by subculturists, but by the reaction they provoke in a given social context. Studying small groups such as Little League baseball teams, Gary Fine (1979: 734) developed the notion of **idioculture**, defined as "a system of knowledge, beliefs, behaviors, and customs shared by members of an interacting group to which members can refer and employ as the basis of further interaction." While applicable to all sorts of small groupings, idioculture reminds us that, rather than being static "things" or formal "groups," subcultures are networks of ongoing, observable *interaction*.

These early waves of American scholarship made a number of important advances relative to subculture studies, including:

- the importance of systematic study, especially fieldwork and participant observation and including seeking subculturists' subjective understandings of what they do;

- the insight that subcultures emerge from *social circumstances* rather than *psychological failings* or group pathologies;
- authorities often label subculturists a criminal or moral threat, leading to broader stigmatization.

While both the theoretical and methodological insights of the Chicago School continue to resonate in subculture studies, social ecology is *too* deterministic, suggesting that subcultural participation is a direct result of social surroundings. Additionally, the focus on crime, social disorganization, and delinquency paints subcultures as social problems rather than diverse, meaningful social spaces.

BIRMINGHAM SCHOOL – STYLE AND SOCIAL CLASS

Like the Chicago School, the Birmingham School recognized the importance of social context in the formation of subcultures. In the decades following World War II, youth cultures exploded in numbers for a variety of reasons: expansions in education created greater space between youth and adult responsibilities; the growth of film, television, and music industries increased youths' exposure to pop culture and alternative ideas; an expanding middle class led to greater disposable income and leisure time; and marketers and parents came to see "teenagers" as a leisure class. Yet not all youth shared in the prosperity of middle-class families and wealth and income disparities persisted (and often *grew*). The relative expansion of the middle class in the postwar years quickly gave way to deindustrialization and urban decline, and eventually the conservative regimes of Margaret Thatcher and Ronald Reagan would undermine the social safety net and accelerate free-market capitalism. In the United Kingdom, scholars associated with the Centre for Contemporary Cultural Studies (CCCS) at the University of Birmingham studied youth during this time of transition, including many of the "classic" subcultures such as mods and punks.

Social class is perhaps *the* central theme of CCCS subcultural studies. Working-class youth (mainly boys) join together by virtue of their marginalization from and resistance to the class structure. Subcultures therefore are primarily working class phenomena, a reworking of the class struggle that had been occurring for generations. In fact, the history of subcultures follows the evolution of working-class styles and identities in the UK, beginning with the teddy boys and leading to the mods and the rockers, skinheads, punks, football hooligans, and more recently "chavs." Anticipating the decline of traditional working-class life, these subculturists engaged in an ideological battle. Capitalist society produces not only economic exploitation and domination, but *cultural* domination. The capitalist class dominates workers not via force of arms (although when necessary they do that, too) but through **cultural hegemony**, in effect creating an ideology that legitimizes their lofty social position and wealth (Gramsci 1971). For example, the notion that one may suffer indignities on earth but find salvation in the afterlife, or the depiction of immigrants as the "enemy" of workers serves the interests of the capitalist class, keeping workers' focus anywhere but on the source of their exploitation. Most especially, the belief that people succeed or fail by their own merits, that the wealthy have *earned* their riches honestly and the poor simply have not tried hard enough, makes class inequality seem natural.

For the CCCS, subcultural identities and resistance were most visible through spectacular youth styles and rituals. Theories of "mass culture" suggested that prefabricated, shallow, homogenizing, lowest-common-denominator cultural forms pacify people into complacency or even submission, reinforcing the hegemony I just discussed (Adorno 1991). In contrast, the CCCS held that people take and remake cultural texts as a form of *resistance*. A pivotal book to emerge from the CCCS was Stuart Hall and Tony Jefferson's edited collection *Resistance Through Rituals* (1976), an examination of the various post war British subcultures such as teddy boys, mods, skinheads, rude boys, and drug-users. Working-class subculturists consumed various elements of pop culture, yes, but they twisted the meanings in subversive ways (see Chapter 3).

Another of the important books to emerge from the CCCS, indeed one of the most cited works in all of subcultural studies, is Dick Hebdige's 1979 *Subculture: The Meaning of Style*. Hebdige saw subcultural style as a **bricolage**, or combination and remaking of various cultural objects; subculturists took ordinary items and transformed their meaning, a famous example being the safety pin that for a punk becomes a lip- or ear-piercing. As the title implies, **style** – in the form of clothing, but also demeanor and argot – constitutes subcultures' distinguishing feature. Subcultures became associated with "spectacular" styles, adherents intentionally making a spectacle of themselves. Stylistic codes simultaneously served two purposes, to set participants apart from "normal" society (and other subcultures) and to establish a particular subcultural identity. Understanding subcultures then involved decoding their style. Subcultural style follows a certain **homology**, or a synergy with a group's values and behavior - skinheads' steel-toed boots, shaved heads, masculine posturing, and love of beer naturally "fit" with their working-class origins and the context of economic decline. Punk style was essentially meaningless "noise," reflecting their "no future" attitude (Hebdige 1979).

Other CCCS scholars such as Stanley Cohen (2002 [1972]) carefully studied public responses to subcultures, developing the concept of **moral panics** to explain the media-generated over-reaction to subcultural "threats" (more on this in Chapter 6). Subculturists became folk devils, blamed for a variety of social ills and symbolizing moral decline. Paul Willis (1977) made important ethnographic and theoretical contributions, studying how the structural position of working class "lads" led them to disdain academics and screw around in school, ultimately ensuring they would remain in working class jobs. Angela McRobbie and Jennie Garber (1976) explored the worlds of young women pop music fans and how they built meaningful communities as they listened to music and pored over teen magazines in "bedroom cultures."

The key contributions in subcultural studies made by British scholars during this period include:

- subcultures emerge primarily among working-class youth collectively resisting structural impediments to upward mobility;
- spectacular styles held ideological meaning beyond mere fashion;
- such styles constituted a symbolic form of resistance;
- authorities and the media create moral panics; and finally
- such resistance is largely ineffectual, as subcultural style itself is eventually coopted and commodified.

However, the CCCS became the foil for new generations of scholars who critiqued these tenets for their overemphasis on class, excessive emphasis on and misreading of style, lack of attention to women and girls' experience, and armchair theorizing of youth with whom they had little direct contact (with some exceptions such as Paul Willis (1977, 1978)). What, in fact, do subculturists *do* and how do *they* make sense of their lives?

POST-SUBCULTURE STUDIES – CLUBCULTURES, SCENES, AND TRIBES

By the early 1990s, many of the classic "underground" sub-cultures – skinhead, punk, metal – seemed to be hollow representations of their original incarnations, replaced by "grunge" scenes and a resurgence of dance cultures. Raves, all-night underground electronic dance music parties fuelled by drugs such as ecstasy, brought together diverse crowds focused more on hedonistic escape than class resistance (see Anderson 2009). In fact, social class, gender, and race seemed less salient, less central to the formation of such scenes. Likewise, rave styles drew from many sources and did not cohere into a rave "uniform." Finally, while rave certainly spawned communities, they seemed diffuse when compared to gangs of mods or groups of punks. In this context, scholars such as Steve Redhead of Manchester Metropolitan University saw subcultures through a postmodern lens, critiquing the "heroic" vision of subculturists as culture warriors. The post-subcultural generation blended all sorts of music and fashion as individuals consumed and created their own styles (Redhead 1997), shopping for fashions *and* identities in a **supermarket of style** (Polhemus 1998). Youth groupings, in the form of scenes or neo-tribes, emerge amid a fragmented culture in which identity becomes unhitched from family, geography, and tradition (see Chapter 2). In a postmodern world, individuals consume and create their own styles. They are less interested in adopting a collective identity, more passionate about pursuing their own creativity and pleasure, drawing from a variety of sources to patch together their own lifestyles (Chaney 2004). In fact, what we call mainstream society is simply a collection of lifestyle clusters, eliminating the difference between so-called subcultures and the rest of society: "[T]he once-accepted distinction between 'sub' and 'dominant' culture can no longer be said to hold true in a world where the so-called dominant culture has fragmented into a plurality of lifestyle sensibilities and preferences" (Chaney 2004: 47).

Reflecting their postmodernist bent, clubculture and post-subculture theories critiqued the very idea of stable, coherent, recognizable subcultures, suggesting that youth formations are fragmented and fluid, better described as scenes (Straw 1991). **Scenes** are "places devoted to practices of meaning making through the pleasures of sociable consumption" (Silver et al. 2010). "Alternative" music, especially grunge, claimed to eschew style entirely, and few talked about grunge as a subculture – in fact, there were few, if any, self-identified "grungers!" The boundaries between scenes are quite porous. In other words, scenes share styles, interests, music, and so on, making it difficult if not impossible to identify distinct groups such as "punks" and "goths." Juggalos, diehard fans of the hardcore rap duo Insane Clown Posse, sometimes have a distinct style, including ICP clothing, tattoos, braids, and the group's trademark scary clown face paint. They share basic values revolving around partying, and gather for concerts and festivals. But in many ways, Juggalos are an amalgam of various scenes – hip hop, metal, goth, punk, emo, even, in some ways, hippies. While they describe themselves as a "family" and unite around their shared alienation from dominant culture, Juggalos are an exceptionally diverse group of people. Furthermore, participation is less consistent. Rather than calling such cultural groupings subcultures, Andy Bennett (1999, 2005) suggests they are better described as **neo-tribes**, diffuse collections of people that gather intermittently, primarily to have a good time, and share some sense of collective identity. This notion seems to perfectly capture rave and other dance cultures' – people gather, but do not share much in the way of an underlying identity or ideology.

A variety of contemporary cultural groupings seem to fit the post-subculturist depiction of youth scenes. Even with the decline of classic raves, electronic dance music scenes continue to thrive, both in clubs and at periodic gatherings such as the Electric Daisy Carnival, an annual festival drawing hundreds of thousands of people. Burning Man, a yearly event held in Nevada's Black Rock Desert, features eclectic art, music, and styles, as 50,000 attendees plan, build, and then dismantle a radical community, complete with a "temple" and a giant wooden effigy (*the* burning man). They cooperatively build large art projects and structures, make music, and trade goods – organizers allow no monetary exchange. While participants share principles of creativity, inclusivity, self-reliance, and decommodification, they do not share a particular subcultural identity. While they naturally forge meaningful relationships, they do not form the consistent, stable bonds or ongoing communities implied in the CCCS vision of subcultures.

Post-subculture theorists emphasize even more than the CCCS the centrality of **consumption** and leisure in alternative cultures; consuming a lifestyle trumps politics or a coherent worldview for many participants. Japan's kogal culture involves young women who in many respects resemble California's "Valley girls": sun-tan, miniskirt, platform shoes, designer handbags, and lots of makeup. The media often dismisses kogals – defined by their conspicuous consumption – as a meaningless fashion trend, even as the girls challenge norms of young Japanese femininity and propriety (Miller 2004). The steampunk subculture, a retro-futurist fandom of Victorian science fiction, professes little in the way of core values beyond a critique of our relationships to contemporary technology and an appreciation for simpler mechanical devices. Participants re-enact an anachronistic version of possible futures as seen through the eyes of the Victorian era, combining corsets, top hats, and goggles with clockwork devices, brass gears, and dials and gauges (VanderMeer 2011). Participants promote an inclusive community, so much so that they struggle even to define steampunk (Cohan 2012). Some identify with a philosophical reinterpretation of technology or DIY activism, but many simply enjoy the *aesthetic*, constructing DIY costumes and retrofitting contemporary technology (e.g. cell phones, keyboards) with brass and gears. Rather than an easily-defined, consistent, coherent subculture of working class youth defined by their resistance, steampunks are more a neo-tribe of shared interests, defined in large part by their consumption.

The central contributions to subcultural (or scene) studies made by scholars during this period include:

- contemporary scenes emerge into a postmodern context, a fragmented culture in which identity is "unmoored" from ascribed characteristics such as race, class, family, and place. Scenes reflect trends towards multiculturalism, commodification, and diffuse boundaries present in the larger world;
- subcultural participation is more a matter of *choice* than a result of structurally determined social positions;
- scene identity and participation are fluid; few people "commit" to a subcultural identity for any length of time;

- consumerism, rather than resistance, and pleasure, rather than politics, better characterize contemporary scenes;
- there is no coherent, identifiable "mainstream" culture, no clear boundary between scenes and a "hegemonic" social order.

However, in many ways the post-subculture argument goes too far. Many people *do* identify with particular cultural groupings and do consistently participate, self-identifying as goths, punks, skaters, and so on (see Hodkinson 2002). While the CCCS overemphasized social class, class does remain a significant element of at least some subcultural participation, and although the CCCS overplayed subcultures' potential political significance, post-subculturists often go too far in the opposite direction (Shildrick and MacDonald 2006). Subcultures may be consumerist, but that does not eliminate their potential for resistance (Blackman 2005).

CONTEMPORARY WORK

A new generation of scholars came of age in the 1980s and 90s as many subcultures – punk, metal, goth, riot grrrl, rave, hip hop, skating, and so on – were emerging or undergoing a resurgence of popularity. Often equipped with firsthand experience in youthful scenes, they pursued advanced degrees in the midst of deepening critiques of the CCCS and the emergence of post-subculture studies. Many such scholars, including Sarah Thornton, conducted Chicago School-inspired ethnographies among the groups in which they grew up. For example Paul Hodkinson's and Dunja Brill's studies of goths; S. Craig Watkins's analysis of hip hop; Lauraine Leblanc's study of punk; Tammy Anderson's work on electronic dance music/rave; Keith Kahn-Harris's study of extreme metal; Kristin Schilt's work on riot grrrl; Christine Feldman's examination of mods; Ryan Moore's analysis of contemporary US music scenes and Rupa Huq's engagement of bhangra and britpop; and my and Patrick Williams' work on straight edge. Bound neither by the CCCS focus on class and marginalization nor by the post-subculturist notion that distinct, coherent subcultures may not exist, these scholars seek a deep understanding of subculturists' experiences *from participants' subjective points of view*, studying via participant observation what subculturists actually *do*. While often sympathetic to subculturists' efforts to "resist" the mainstream, they also offer critical analyses of the contradictions and inequalities reproduced in scenes. Moving beyond an exclusive focus on social class, they often explain how participants challenge and reinforce social norms surrounding gender and sexuality. Subcultures become **strategies**, sets of micro-level practices embedded within social structures (more on this in Chapter 2). Further, given the rise of digital media, such scholars have paid special attention to the *virtual* and *mediated* aspects of subcultures. Finally, while the connections between subculture studies and music/pop culture remain strong, some writers are deploying subcultural concepts in new territories, including Jeff Kidder's (2011) study of bike messengers and Amy Best's (2006) work on car cultures.

Many US scholars, especially, draw upon the theoretical traditions developed by Chicago School-inspired theorists such as Howard Becker and Erving Goffman, adopting a **symbolic interactionist** approach to investigate subculturists' lived experiences. Ironically writing around the same time as Dick Hebdige (1979), Gary Alan Fine and Sherryl Kleinman (1979) anticipated many of the post-subculture scholars' critiques of the CCCS. Rather than stable groups with recognizable "members," clear boundaries, and universal core values, subcultures are meaning systems that constantly change, have diverse participants, and are among the many micro-cultures participants inhabit. The various participants do not themselves constitute the subculture.

Contemporary work on subcultures does not constitute a coherent "school" of thought, but draws upon the strengths of each previous strand of scholarship. Some of the main themes in current research include:

- attention to participants' subjective understandings of their activities, often through ethnographic or interview studies;
- focus on the nuanced and multiple *meanings* subculturists construct, reflecting the symbolic interactionist emphasis on everyday lived experience, and likewise viewing subcultural involvement as an intentional, reflexive *strategy* to grapple with personal and collective challenges;
- further attention to how race, class, gender, and sexuality shape subcultural experience;

- attending to the role of digital media, as subculturists increasingly participate partly or completely online;
- increasing interest in disconnecting subculture from youth and instead examining subcultural activity across the life course.

Of course this latest round of thinking no doubt has its own shortcomings, weaknesses that will gradually become more apparent. Despite the diversity of contemporary subculture studies, one might argue that scholars remain too focused on youth and on music, that they neglect rural scenes in favor of urban, and that at times are too focused on micro-interactions and meanings at the expense of grasping larger structural contexts.

A WORKING DEFINITION: WHAT "COUNTS" AS A SUBCULTURE?

Even given the history of what has come to be called subculture studies, the question still remains: just what is a subculture? Are surfers a subculture? Strippers? Immigrants? Collectors of child pornography? Perhaps as scholar Michael Clarke (1974) once suggested, the concept has been used so indiscriminately and uncritically that it may be useless. Part of the struggle with defining an object of study is striking a balance between employing a concept too narrowly or, alternately, too broadly. In other words, too narrow a concept may exclude phenomena and miss the diversity of human experience, but defined too broadly a concept quickly becomes irrelevant or meaningless. "Subcultures" are not static "things" but rather a way we describe and understand the ongoing processes of segments and moments of social life.

Employing a very broad understanding of subcultures, we might think of them simply as smaller "pieces" of a larger culture or society, differing in some way from "mainstream" culture (see Gordon 1947). Following this line of thinking, knitting circles and skinheads might both qualify. However, such an inclusive definition is not very useful. First, cultures are not "blocks" of people and their ways of life, to be broken up into smaller sections, but rather ever-changing symbolic blueprints that guide and give meaning to people's beliefs, values, behaviors, and material things. Second, such a wide-ranging conceptualization of subculture includes social experiences and groups so diverse that they bear little resemblance to one another;

Buddhists and gun collectors might be empirically different enough that one concept cannot adequately explain them. Finally, if we describe *any* social grouping as a subculture, the concept *does* become virtually useless. A concept is only useful if it offers some way of describing and distinguishing social phenomena from other another.

Placing too narrow boundaries around the concept of subculture also comes with pitfalls. Are vegans a subculture, social movement, lifestyle, or counterculture? Depending upon what aspect(s) of veganism one deems most important, one could make an argument for each of these concepts. And various vegans may describe themselves, their identities, and their practices in ways that fit any of these categories, or even more than one. The point: concepts will overlap, and social phenomena may cut across our definitions. Rather than identifying concrete criteria by which we judge a social grouping a subculture or not, it is more useful to discuss the significant characteristics as continua and thereby discuss a grouping's "subcultureness." So, a working definition:

> **SUBCULTURE:** A *relatively diffuse* social network having a *shared identity, distinctive meanings* around certain ideas, practices, and objects, and a sense of *marginalization* from or *resistance* to a perceived "conventional" society.

Let's briefly examine each element of this definition.

Diffuse networks. First, subculture describes the patterns of experience and the connections between people engaged in ongoing interaction. They have symbolic boundaries, but as post-subculture theorists insist, those boundaries are diffuse, with individuals coming and going and with few absolute markers of belonging (Hodkinson 2002). Subcultures (or scenes, or neo-tribes) have relatively little (if any) *formal* leadership, bureaucratic organizational structure, membership lists, or rationally-planned, legitimated rules as compared to conventional businesses, schools, political parties, and civic groups.

Shared identity. Similarly, participants in a particular subculture identify with one another and see themselves as different from others, including, often, other subculturists. In other words, they recognize one another, even if not immediately, and they feel some connection to a subcultural identity, other subculturists, or both. Behaviors and styles alone do not constitute a subculture; not just anyone with a tattoo is part of the body modification *subculture*, which requires those tattoos to be a central part of one's identity.

Shared distinctive meanings. Subculturists share ideas (e.g. values and beliefs), practices (e.g. rituals and leisure), and objects (e.g. skateboards, steel-toed boots) (Williams 2011). Subculturists do not simply inherit or "join" a preexisting set of meanings, but actively create them. Not at all does this mean that all adherents of a particular subculture share identical understandings of these things; in fact, participants regularly *contest* meanings. Still, they recognize these objects' significance and the subcultural meanings they entail. To some degree, these meanings are distinct from widely accepted norms and values, that is they deviate from the norm, making them different from "lifestyles" (see below). Subcultures are in some way non-normative.

Resistance. Subculturists tend to offer, either passively or actively, some sort of resistance to "mainstream," dominant, or hegemonic culture (see Chapter 3). As I showed above, scholars hotly debate the importance of resistance. To varying degrees, subcultures foster an oppositional consciousness or even an "intentionally antagonistic relationship with normal society" (Williams 2011: 3). Subculturists "band together based on a shared set of values or beliefs and *deny, resist, or stray from* those commonly held by the mainstream culture overall" (Greenberg 2007: xvi). Men's fraternal organizations such as the Elks or Lions may share meanings and identity, but they hardly oppose dominant practices (and in fact, likely reinforce patriarchy and class differences).

Marginalization. Finally, and significantly, subculturists share a degree of outsider status even as they are rarely completely distinct or separate from other social groups. Many, maybe even most, contemporary subculturists are not *structurally* marginalized but rather in a sense "choose" their marginalization. Presumably, no one forces someone to adopt a goth identity, yet that chosen identity marks one as an outsider, even potentially generating social stigma. Cheerleaders might constitute diffuse networks of young women, certainly share meanings around certain objects and practices, but are rarely marginalized.

Again, a subculture is not a "thing," not an immediately recognizable "group," but rather a set of diverse meanings and practices that change over time. The athletes at US universities may have a distinctive lifestyle and may even feel marginalized (often around race). However, they do not constitute a subculture under my conceptualization. Athletes are not a coherent category of people; while there may be trends and patterns among athletes, by and large their values and motivations mirror those of the dominant culture. Likewise, police may inhabit idiocultures replete with distinctive norms and practices, but their investment in the dominant social order – upholding laws, a primary expression of dominant values – excludes them from my definition.

DOING SUBCULTURE – COMMON PRACTICES

In addition to the basic characteristics outlined above, many subcultures also share:

- **Specialized vocabulary:** many subcultures have a distinctive, shared vernacular of idioms and symbols that demonstrate belonging and insider knowledge, marking those "in the know" from outsiders. For example, graffiti writers commonly talk about crews, bombing, tags, throw-ups, to get up, burn, and wildstyle.
- **Style and music:** many, but not all, subcultures feature connections to particular music styles and fashions. Both serve as vehicles of self-expression and collective opposition.
- **Subcultural history or lore:** most subculturists have a sense of their history (in fact, knowing about a subculture's "roots" can be a way of performing and judging authenticity). Certain events become legendary – the bank holiday riots in the UK, the Woodstock and Altamont rock concerts in the US, the first Wacken Open Air metal festival in Germany. Subcultural history, like history in general, is often written around people of significance – heroes, innovators, and pioneers. The body modification and "modern primitive" scenes honor Fakir Musafar as an early inspiration, while "Sailor Jerry" Collins, a prominent tattoo artist in Hawaii until his death in 1973, remains a legend in the tattoo world.
- **Social support system:** due to their deviant identities and practices, many subcultures serve as social support systems, refuges or "homes" where likeminded people feel accepted. Subculturists may even become chosen *families*, forming significant, long-term bonds.

BUT WHAT ABOUT GANGS? SUBCULTURES IN RELATION TO OTHER SOCIAL GROUPINGS

Even with a working definition, you still might wonder just what "counts" as a subculture and what does not. Conceptually, subcultures have much in common with other social groupings, including countercultures, gangs, social movements, lifestyles, new religious movements, and fan cultures. Scholars (and sometimes participants) hotly contest the meaning and usefulness of *all* of these concepts, but each of them potentially has an element of subcultureness.

LIFESTYLES

A **lifestyle** is "any distinctive … mode of living" (Sobel 1981: 3) including people's tastes, the way they dress and talk, what they buy, their dietary choices, their hobbies or other interests and so on. A lifestyle encompasses one's personal self-expression, an attempt to distinguish oneself from others. Those advocating a post-subculture conceptualization emphasize the apolitical leisure and consumerist orientation of youth scenes – kids just want to have fun! Clearly subculturists are practicing various lifestyles, but conceptually, subcultural norms, values, and practices are more oppositional or deviant than the average lifestyle. People living an "upper class" lifestyle might decorate their home with expensive antiques, drink fine wine, and drive expensive cars, but they are hardly subcultural. Likewise, a regular practitioner of yoga might learn its history and philosophy in addition to difficult poses, thereby identifying deeply with yoga and other yoga devotees, but yoga is widely accepted by the general public and not so different from other efforts at self-improvement.

SOCIAL MOVEMENTS

Broadly speaking, **social movements** are organized, collective, manifestly political, public challenges made against "authority structures," typically government bodies (McAdam et al. 2001). Discussions of social movements evoke images of activists parading through the streets, committing civil disobedience, or clashing with police as they struggle for new corporate or government policies – anti-war, environmental, human rights, global democracy, and the

"Arab Uprising" movements serving as prime examples. Still, social movements and subcultures share common ground. Like sub-cultures, "new" social movements such as animal rights, feminist, and queer movements contest dominant cultural norms in addition to fighting for political rights. Yet social movement scholars focus most on "contentious politics," collective protest efforts to change public policy. Certainly subculturists *do* participate in protest movements – Occupy protests against economic inequality from New York to Sydney included street punks and other subcultural youth alongside more conventional students and others. However, *relative to subcultures*, social movements feature greater organization, more consistent focus on social change, more frequent (often con-tentious) public interactions with the state, and often (although not always) a more coherent political worldview, including specific goals and a vision for the future (more on this in Chapter 3).

COUNTERCULTURES

Countercultures involve extrainstitutional challenges to *cultural* authorities. Theodor Roznak (1969/1995) used the term counter-culture to describe the youth cultures of the 1960s. Counterculture seems to fill the conceptual gap between social movement and subculture, more culturally oriented and less formally organized than many movements, but more change oriented and oppositional than many subcultures (see Haenfler 2013). J. Milton Yinger (1960) distinguished between "contracultures" in conflict with dominant society and subcultures, groups with distinctive norms that may or may not openly conflict with the larger culture. They place a premium on individuality, having perhaps even less coherence than many subcultures. Observing "The Counterculture" of the 1960s, Roznak noted a broad rejection of "technocratic society" and championing of creativity and self-fulfillment, exemplified by the hippies.

NEW RELIGIOUS MOVEMENTS

Some religious groups that fall outside the mainstream world faiths seem subcultural, including Falun Gong, a contemporary Chinese movement known for its slow, meditative exercises and peaceful philosophy, and Wicca, a pagan faith whose practitioners perform ceremonial magic in honor of both a goddess and a god. **New religious movements** (NRMs) are contemporary religious, spiritual, or philosophical entities that differ significantly from (but are often related to) the world's major established religions (Cowan and Bromley 2007). Like subcultures, members of NRMs have distinctive norms and practices and are therefore often marginalized; political and religious authorities often brand them as "cults." For example, the Chinese government severely persecuted Falun Gong, even torturing some adherents to death, and Hare Krishnas, whose devotees are recognizable by their orange robes and topknot of hair, have faced accusations of brainwashing recruits. However, NRMs are often somewhat more organized than subcultures, and more importantly, their emphasis on the spiritual or supernatural make them distinctive enough to warrant their own concept.

GANGS

Typically composed of marginalized youth who form communities for protection and criminal enterprise, gangs are in many ways subcultural. After all, Chicago School researchers such as Frederic Thrasher and William Foote Whyte (and later, Albert Cohen) studied delinquent youth often described as gangs. Gang members have norms, codes, and practices that distinguish them from the more conventional world. Mara Salvatrucha (MS-13), a gang with tens of thousands of members in Central and North America, has a secretive language composed of hand signs and uses tattoos to differentiate members from other gangs. Gangs, like subcultures, spend a good bit of their time pursuing leisure (e.g. partying) and engaging in various types of deviance. Still, grouping a violent criminal organization such as MS-13, known for kidnapping, human trafficking, and brutal murders, with a spectacular subculture such as goth stretches the utility of both concepts. Some gangs, particularly those engaged in ongoing criminal activities, have more formal structure than most subcultures. The Yakuza in Japan have elaborate subcultural rituals and tattoos but their strict, formal hierarchy means they are better described as an organized criminal group than a subculture. Further, despite being national and even international, at the local level gangs often have a greater focus on territoriality than many contemporary subcultures. Finally, while scholars argue about the centrality of crime in definitions of gangs, many agree that criminality is a central feature of contemporary gangs, and this is even truer in popular discourse and among law enforcement. While participants in subcultures may occasionally break the law, crime is less central to their existence.

FAN CULTURES/FANDOMS

Finally, subcultures certainly overlap with **fan cultures** or **fandoms**, described by Henry Jenkins as communities who share a deep interest in some object of popular culture and who translate their love into cultural activity with other fans. Fandoms are **participatory cultures**, that is rather than being passive media consumers fans appropriate the object of their fandom, creating their own stories, films, and fashions, often with subversive twists (Jenkins 2006). Fans of *Star Trek*, *Star Wars*, *Doctor Who*, *Sailor Moon*, and Bollywood or martial arts films might make their own fan films, write fan fiction, or create costumes. Fandoms and subcultures share much in common: non-normative or deviant activities; an emphasis on authenticity among participants (e.g. "true" fans, and "true" punks); and an amateur, often underground network for sharing creativity (e.g. fan fiction sites and 'zines) (see Hills 2002). Some fan cultures are quite subcultural. Football (soccer) clubs' supporters (fans) around the world share an almost tribal identity, not just attending matches together but fighting other clubs' fans (firms) and creating general mayhem in the terraces (Frosdick and Marsh 2005). Such supporters, called "football hooligans" by the press, are not your everyday fans; in many ways, being part of a football firm is a deviant way of life. Other fandoms seem too benign to be accurately described as subcultures. Fans of the *Twilight* series may, on average, be relatively less deviant than many subculturists; they are hardly marginalized or resistant, their difference ending with an abiding interest in pop culture.

I'll make one last warning *against* insisting on too limiting a definition of subculture and *for* recognizing that many of the concepts I've just discussed overlap. Skateboarding is variously a professional sport, a commodified lifestyle, and, particularly in its less visible forms, a subculture. Not every person who skates identifies with the

Table 1.1

Lifestyle	Social movement	Counterculture	New religious movement	Gang	Fan culture	Subculture
Fitness	Civil rights	Communes	Wicca	Crips/Bloods	Anime	Skinhead/mod
Surfing	Feminist	kibbutz	Asatru	Wah Ching	Harry Potter	graffiti writers
Raw food diet	Peace	Hippies	Scientology	MS-13	Twilight	Skaters
Backpackers	Animal rights	Green living	Falun Gong	Aryan	Soccer fans	Punk/straight
Vegetarians	Labour	Queer Cultures	Bahá'í	Brotherhood	Star Wars/	edge
Swingers	Environmental	New age	Hare Krishna	Yardie gangs	Star Trek	Riot Grrl

skater subculture; an otherwise conventional kid may enjoy skating but not relate to skaters' more subversive values. But for some, skating infuses much of their lives beyond riding a skateboard, influencing their friendship circles, music, and fashion, but also encouraging an anti-authoritarian ethos and opposition to commodified skating.

WHY STUDY SUBCULTURES?

Subcultures may sometimes seem weird, gross, dangerous, or silly, but I believe we should take them seriously and that they deserve serious study. Subcultures have ushered generations of youth into adulthood, providing affirming spaces for kids who otherwise feel like aliens among their peers and fostering non-normative values they often take with them as they grow. Sometimes adults forget just how brutal middle and high school can be on kids whom for one or another reason don't fit in. Rather than causing *problems*, subcultures often provide *solutions* for troubled kids in the form of meaningful community.

I can certainly attest to subcultures' transformative potential. Punk rock gave me permission, even encouragement, to question everything and to regard authority with suspicion. The metalheads in my high school made it OK that I couldn't afford fancy clothes, while the music changed my thinking about war, political power, and fundamentalist religion. Rap group NWA's infamous track "Fuck tha Police" was more than a naughty song, it alerted me to police brutality and urban violence, while Public Enemy's "Black Steel in the Hour of Chaos" taught me something about racism and the prison industrial complex. Seeing queercore bands Tribe 8 and Spitboy aggressively challenge homophobia and patriarchy blew my mind and gave me a sense of responsibility to fight oppressions of all kinds. It is no exaggeration to say that hardcore and straight edge profoundly impacted my diet, my style, my friendship circles, even my career path. And yes, each of these scenes was *fun*! As subculturists age, they carry some of subcultural ideas and practices with them. Subcultural identities often resonate into adulthood, and many of those adults go on to shape other social institutions, becoming teachers, businesspeople, artists and musicians, even politicians. They get jobs, vote, and have children of their own. In short, subcultures impact our larger social worlds.

Subcultures are also important because they tell us something about our society at large. In their opposition, they reflect back at us our hypocrisies, forcing us to ask "oppositional to *what?*" Conformity? Racism? Intolerance? Violence? Hyper-consumption? Beauty standards? Subculturists may not be heroes, but if we listen, they may teach *us* something.

KEY INSIGHTS

- Subcultures do not objectively exist; they are not coherent, easily identifiable groups with stable memberships and clear boundaries. Subculture is simply a concept we use to describe a set of ongoing social relationships and the meanings people give to the experiences and objects involved. Therefore while we use the term subculture for ease of discussion, it may be more accurate to think of such phenomena as *subcultural.*
- While giving a strict conceptual definition of subculture is neither possible nor desirable, several common characteristics encapsulate *subcultural* experience. Importantly, subculturists share a sense of *marginalization* from or *resistance* to a perceived "conventional" society.
- Subcultures can have much in common with – but are conceptually distinct from – lifestyles, social movements, countercultures, new religious movements, gangs, and fandoms.
- Scholars have framed subcultures by social class (participants are working class), gender (male), age (youth), race (immigrant, ethnic, minority), and delinquency (engaged in criminal activity). As I will argue in later chapters, *none* of these characteristics defines subculture as a concept.

EXPLORING FURTHER

Subcultural Theory: Traditions and Concepts, by J. Patrick Williams, 2011 (Polity). This book offers a more advanced discussion of subcultural theory for readers who really want to wrestle with the nuances of the field.

The Post-Subcultures Reader, edited by David Muggleton and Rupert Weinzierl, 2003 (Berg). These essays explore various international scenes from the post-subculture critique, offering a thorough explanation of post-subculture studies.

Goths, Gamers, and Grrrls: Deviance and Youth Subcultures (2nd edn), by Ross Haenfler, 2012 (Oxford University Press). This book integrates deviance and subculture studies, each chapter using a youth culture – for example, skinheads, gamers, and virginity pledgers – to explore key concepts in both fields.

After Subculture: Critical Studies in Contemporary Youth Culture, edited by Andy Bennett and Keith Kahn-Harris, 2004 (Palgrave). A collection of authors writing about a variety of scenes, but all grappling with questions surrounding the subculture and post-subculture debate.

Subculture: The Meaning of Style, by Dick Hebdige, 1979 (Methuen). While many of Hebdige's ideas have received intense criticism, this book remains a key touchstone in subculture studies.

Club Cultures: Music, Media, and Subcultural Capital, by Sarah Thornton, 1995 (Polity). One of the most important subculture studies of the 1990s, taking an insider perspective to explore how subculturists enact distinction.

Youth Cultures: Scenes, Subcultures, and Tribes, edited by Paul Hodkinson and Wolfgang Deicke, 2007 (Routledge). A collection of papers on a variety of subcultures/scenes addressing a range of issues across the theoretical schools discussed in this chapter.

"Subcultures and Post-Subcultures: Researching Contemporary Youth," lecture on the conceptual history of subculture delivered by leading music sociologist and youth culture scholar Andy Bennett at Tallinn University in 2012. http://vimeo.com/41696336

Electric Daisy Carnival Experience, directed by Kevin Kerslake, 2011. Documentary about the Electric Daisy electronic dance music festival in Las Vegas, Nevada. Illustrates the "neo-tribal" nature of some youth cultures.

2

HOW DO SUBCULTURES EMERGE AND WHY DO PEOPLE PARTICIPATE?

Adults often treat youth as a *problem* to be managed, alternating efforts to curb underage drinking, teen-pregnancy, and juvenile delinquency with prescriptions to cure depression, eating disorders, and low self-esteem. A headline in the satirical newspaper *The Onion* reads "Area Teen Up to Something," the story noting "Signs that the teenager may be up to no good have so far included his hunched over posture, the way he keeps looking around with his eyes, and the fact that he probably owns a number of those violent video games." The article pokes fun at adults' tendency to view "strange" young people with a mixture of wonder, suspicion, and even fear, but the satire works because many times this is the case. Given that most people associate subcultures with youth, the same wariness applies, compounded by media stereotypes of sub-culturists as troubled, alienated, delinquent, or violent kids. Thus a central concern for adults, including many scholars, has been to explain just why young people would "join" subcultures, often with the aim of curtailing deviance and delinquency.

In this chapter, I take on several related questions. First, how do subcultures emerge? What social contexts and time periods facilitate subcultural activities and identities? Then, at the individual level, I ask, "Why do people participate," challenging popular conceptions of subculturalists as universally alienated, delinquent, or psychologically troubled youth.

HOW DO SUBCULTURES EMERGE?

When social groups were smaller and more homogenous, there were fewer subcultures as we understand them today. My parents grew up during the 1950s in a small South Dakota town called Avon of about 600 people. While there were certainly cliques and interest groups, the community was very homogenous. People shared basic values, went to Protestant churches on Sunday, were mostly whites of German descent, and many farmed or were in other ways connected to agriculture. The internet and cable television didn't exist; entertainment revolved around family gatherings, school functions, church events, and the occasional drive-in movie. The smallness of the community meant everyone knew everyone else, making the cost of deviance high. If you broke the rules or stood out in any sort of negatively-perceived way, there was nowhere to hide. Geographic isolation and general conformity left little room for subcultures. The same could be said of contemporary hunter-gatherer societies.

While societies have always had subgroups of a sort – warrior classes, guilds, religious sects, kinship clans, even gangs – most of what we now think of as subcultures emerged in the twentieth century, and the emergence of new subcultures seems to have accelerated after World War II. What sorts of changes prompted this explosion of subcultural activity?

MODERNIZATION: HOW DO SUBCULTURES RELATE TO THE MODERN WORLD?

For starters, small, close-knit communities like Avon are increasingly giving way to cosmopolitan, multicultural cities. Whereas my grandparents began their lives without automobiles, telephones, or TVs, rarely travelled more than 30 miles from home, and lived their entire lives in one place, I have moved numerous times, travelled around the world, and in some ways *carry* the entire world in my pocket on my smartphone. For more than a century, social theorists have sought to explain the social changes associated with

modernization, suggesting that the Enlightenment and Industrial Revolution ushered in a new age that radically transformed societies. Among the many massive social shifts include: increasing democracy; a focus on human rights; increasing individualism; science and rational planning replacing religion; and the movement of masses of people from rural to urban areas. Each of these changes, as well as the accelerated pace and greater depth of change, has facilitated the social conditions in which subcultures emerge and thrive.

Most generally, modernization creates more space for people to experiment with a variety of identities (Giddens 1991b). In other words, our identities are in some ways less ascribed, that is, less determined by the families, communities, and societies in which we are born. As an example, if you had been born a serf in medieval Europe, you would remain a serf, your identity and your life more or less proscribed by your social position. Likewise, the caste system of India left little room for social mobility. Religious strictures and political rules made sure people knew their "place." In the modern world, our identities have become unmoored from stable social roles (Gergen 2000). Compared to the past, contemporary life (particularly in rich countries) is fluid; people change jobs, religions, homes, nationalities, husbands/wives, lifestyles, and political ideas (Bauman 2000). This relatively newfound freedom is both gift and burden, a gift in that we are freer to "invent" ourselves, a burden in the sense that who we are, what we become, rests totally on our shoulders. Ulrich Beck and Elizabeth Beck-Gernsheim (2002) argue that individuals in contemporary societies are increasingly responsible for constructing their own lives. This process of **individualization** makes identity work not only possible but also an imperative. If you are not successful, it's a result of your personal shortcomings. Dissatisfied with your body? Go to the gym or get a makeover. If you are unhappy, it's up to you to find a way to be happy. You should *work* to develop a positive self-image. People constantly think about and tinker with their sense of self, picking clothes that reflect a certain image, choosing hairstyles, and reading self-help books to be "better" people. The "self" is a reflexive, ongoing, intentional *process* as well as a *project* (Sandstrom et al. 2009). Is it any wonder that in this context people would find meaning and connection in subcultural identities?

Modernization also facilitated the expansion of **"youth" into a life stage** (see Furlong 2012). While I take care to point out that subcultures are *not* exclusively the domain of the young, many people do begin their subcultural explorations at a young age. We take the notion of "youth" for granted, but it is a relatively modern invention. In the past, children took on adult responsibilities at much younger ages, often apprenticing in a trade or helping out on the family farm early in life. There was little space between childhood and adulthood. Child labor laws, public education, greater productivity and an expansion of the middle classes meant for some an **increase in leisure time**, allowing new generations both the time and money to explore subcultural activities. American marketers created the entire notion of "teenagers" as a new consumer niche after WWII, selling the right to self-determination and pleasure. Now, many parents expect, even *encourage*, their teens to explore various identities and activities while developing their own sense of self. Psychologists see such play as an important stage in the development of independence and a personal self-concept (see Santrock 2011). Subcultures thrive in the liminal space between childhood and adulthood.

I think it is worth noting that the changes of late modernity didn't just "happen" as a result of larger social forces, but that increasing numbers of people began intentionally questioning and challenging the status quo. The 1960s provided the context for an expansive **youth counterculture** fostering "broad criticism or rejection of cultural imperatives – conformity, consumerism, sexual mores, gender roles, religious doctrine" (Haenfler 2013: 1). Self-exploration and spiritual seeking associated with the "new age" movement became more acceptable. Simultaneously, students and other young people protested from London to Paris, Mexico City to San Francisco, as anti-war and other social movements escalated. Minority groups demanded political rights but also vehemently asserted their basic right to *be*. Gay Pride, Black Power, and Women's Liberation all paved the way for increasing numbers of "deviant" subcultures. In the modern world, everyday life is a cultural battleground, a struggle for who we are collectively and individually, a fight for self-determination (Touraine 1981). That struggle takes the form of countercultures, new social movements, and yes, subcultures.

POSTMODERNITY: ARE SUBCULTURES SIMPLY COMMODIFIED IMAGES?

Postmodern theorists argue that the changes brought on by modernity have instigated a profound break from the past characterized by fragmentation, commodification, incoherence, and the primacy of image and spectacle. There may be no coherent explanation for the emergence of subcultures. All we might say is that they are part of a larger social fragmenting and a recycling of the past into meaningless bricolage. Postmodernity inundates us with images and visual images take on ever-greater importance (Baudrillard 1995). In a prescient foreshadowing of the hyperreal future to come, British new wave group The Buggles' recording of "Video Killed the Radio Star" – on their appropriately-titled postmodern record *The Age of Plastic* – was the first song aired by MTV in 1981. The ability to sing seems almost secondary to the *image* a singer must now construct, forging herself into a visually appealing, marketable *brand*. In fact, *everything* is a brand – political parties, religious institutions, universities – and everything is for sale.

In such a context, subcultures emerge as simply another set of images, part of the larger pop culture spectacle amplified by the mass media. The proliferation of subcultures coincides with the triumph of the image. In fact, the media, authorities, and market forces help "create" subcultures in the first place (Thornton 1995). Have you ever heard someone call himself a hipster? Probably not (or only ironically!). Yet according to the media, hipsters are everywhere. Perhaps so-called hipsters constitute a marketing demographic, a set of images for consumption. Consumption is, as both the CCCS and post-subcultural theorists agree, an important part of subcultural experience. We shop for shoes, cars, mobile phone cases and ringtones – why not identities? Religions? News? And why not off-the-rack subcultural personas complete with ready-made rituals and mass-produced accessories available at your local mall? In a postmodern, consumerist culture, subcultures emerge as hollow, manufactured marketing ploys designed to sell images of rebellion – all style and no substance.

Of course we might also suggest that subcultures emerge as a *response* to the conditions of postmodernity, sites of meaning-making and searching for something genuine in a plastic world. In the era of dime-a-dozen pop stars and celebrities famous for nothing – Kim Kardashian, Paris Hilton, the cast of *Jersey Shore* – subcultures may be efforts of resistance.

SOCIAL CONTRADICTIONS: DO SUBCULTURES ATTEMPT TO RESOLVE SOCIETY'S HYPOCRISIES?

By several measures, the twentieth century witnessed an incredible rise in many people's standard of living – better sanitation and medicine produced increased health and longevity, while rising incomes and educational levels created new opportunities for leisure. Yet not everyone shared equally in the gains of the last century and in fact rising expectations were coupled with tremendous inequality. Subcultures arise in response to such **contradictions** in their "parent" cultures (Brake 1985). For example, the class-based resistance of the Birmingham School (discussed in Chapter 1) suggests that working-class youth turn to subcultures in societies that hold out the promise of equal opportunity and affluence while reproducing rampant inequalities. Skinheads valorized the working class even as their way of life declined in the midst of globalization and deindustrialization. We could read graffiti-writing as a response to the contradictions of urban space; modern cities are supposed to be the pinnacle of civilization, yet can also be sterile, ugly, even cruel places. Subcultures emerge to "solve" (even if in an illusory fashion) tensions or problems in society. They teach us something about the flaws of the societies in which they emerge.

Contemporary societies are rife with contradictions related to youth. Parents and educators tell young people to pursue higher education while cutting public support for universities. Democratic nations extol equal opportunity, yet wealth inequality continues to expand. In the US, politicians regularly flaunt their pro-family values, using childhood innocence to frame their agendas even as they do relatively little to support pro-family policies such as maternity/paternity leave, flexible work schedules, and workplace daycare. In fact, the rise of many subcultures since the 1970s coincides with expanding neoliberal policies that champion the free market, deregulation, and privatization against all other values (Moore 2010). The result, as the global financial crisis has so painfully shown, is market volatility, increased uncertainty, and downward mobility, for both working and middle class youth. "[T]he gap between the expectations created by an individualistic culture and the reality of a declining middle class is especially acute for the younger generations" (Moore 2010: 17–18). While punks *sang* about anarchy, "the true source of anarchy in contemporary society is unrestrained capitalism" (Moore 2010: 18).

SHARING, BORROWING, AND REJECTING: SUBCULTURES EMERGE IN REACTION TO OTHER SUBCULTURES?

CCCS scholars saw a more or less chronological lineage shared by working-class youth subcultures. Punks came from skinheads, skinheads from mods, and mods from teddy boys. In other words, each youth subculture emerged, more or less, from the ashes of the old. Such a linear progression is too simplistic – subcultures emerge from a variety of influences and many persist over time – yet subcultures interact with and react to one another. For example, skinheads and punks typically despised and defined themselves in opposition to hippies. New subcultures emerge not only from larger social contradictions but also as responses to *subcultural* contradictions (Haenfler 2006). Hardcore and straight edge emerged as offshoots of a punk scene viewed as too hedonistic and apolitical. Extreme metal (e.g. death metal, black metal) rejected the flamboyant glam or "hair metal" scenes of the mid-1980s. New subcultures, or even new variations, may be **subcultural innovations** in which participants try to improve upon the old, especially attempting to be more "authentic," "original," or "real." Within broad subculture such as hip hop there are many subgroups, with different but overlapping styles, values, practices, and music. Underground, "conscious" scenes may define themselves against more commercial, sexist, consumerist scenes. And as post-subculture theorists point out, scenes borrow extensively from one another, calling into question the very notion of distinct subcultures. Skateboarding, for example, borrows punk, stoner, hip hop and other aesthetics.

WHY DO PEOPLE PARTICIPATE?

I'm not sure my parents ever really understood why as a teenage metalhead I would want to grow my hair longer, listen to bands with names like "Megadeth" and "Slayer," or wear torn jeans and black t-shirts depicting zombies butchering innocent people. No doubt many adults wonder *why* subcultural youth do the things they do, from writing graffiti and using drugs, to piercing and tattooing body parts that should be left well alone. The answer to the question "Why do people participate in subcultures?" is as complicated as why they emerge in the first place, but some explanations are better than others.

PSYCHOLOGICAL EXPLANATIONS: ARE SUBCULTURISTS PSYCHOLOGICALLY DISTURBED?

By virtue of subculturists' "deviant" practices, people commonly believe they are somehow psychologically different from "normal" people – not just different, but damaged. Why else would someone pierce the length of their body with hooks and then suspend themselves by the skin from the ceiling, as participants in the "modern primitive" movement have long done (see Vale and Juno 1989)? Common sense might dictate that they and other subculturists suffer from depression, mood disorders, childhood neglect, or an unhealthy desire for attention. However, when it comes to subcultures, common sense often makes little sense. Even in the case of the most "extreme" subcultures, participants often have fairly rational motivations.

Imagine self-identified vampires who derive pleasure from drinking human blood. Not the sparkling fictional vampires popularized by the *Twilight* book and movie series, or the sun-garlic-and-cross-fearing vamps from old movies, but real people who drink blood from small incisions made on (willing) donors. Many would find the practice revolting and judge the vampires psychologically disturbed, likely suggesting they seek serious therapy. Yet scholar and psychotherapist D. J. Williams' (2008) study of human vampires revealed that most participants were relatively healthy, well-adjusted people who have an interest in "deviant leisure." The subculture, also known as the "Sanguinarium," has a code of ethics (the "Black Veil") centered around safety, consent, valuing diversity, and respecting elders. While drinking blood may seem like a strange way to explore creativity, spirituality, and play, Williams (2009) suggests participants do not act out of psychopathological motivations. As with many subcultures, the Sanguinarium challenges our notions of "normalcy"; in other words, it may not be the vampires who have a problem, but those who rush to prematurely judge them. For perspective, compare the real harm done by a few cuts verses the prevalence of American football players' debilitating head injuries, hurts that until recently players, coaches, and fans took completely for granted as simply "part of the game."

While some subculturists certainly face psychological challenges, savvy psychologists question the notion that subcultures *cause* anti-social behavior. There is some evidence that subculturists actually find respite from social stigma among their peers, that participation actually makes them feel better about themselves. The 1990s saw a panic that listening to heavy metal music led some youth to commit suicide (see Chapter 6). While heavy metal fans may be more likely to attempt suicide, Scheel and Westefeld (1999: 269) report in a study of metalheads that:

> Another compelling focus of further efforts to clarify the relationship between heavy metal music and increased vulnerability to suicide is not the effects of fans' music listening, but broader features of their lives – their families, abilities, hopes, and aspirations, or lack thereof – that may attract some to such negative music.

Metalheads suggest their music helps them deal with their anger (Arnett 1996). Thus rather than identifying with a subculture because they are unstable, people choose these communities to cope with or escape from stresses in other parts of their lives.

STRAIN AND SOCIAL DISORGANIZATION: DO SUBCULTURISTS COME FROM BAD BACKGROUNDS? ARE THEY UP TO NO GOOD?

So, broadly speaking, most subculturists likely do not suffer any more psychological problems than the general population, and in any case, psychological trauma is not a reliable predictor of subcultural participation. But perhaps *social* disruptions – lack of opportunities, run-down schools, "broken" families – contribute to deviant behavior. Returning to our question of why people participate in deviant subcultures, recall from Chapter 1 that the Chicago School found that social disorganization caused by rapid migration and urbanization led to higher rates of deviance and crime. Poverty, run-down neighborhoods, high divorce rates might all lead to **social disorganization** that pushes people into non-normative communities such as subcultures.

Similarly, people might join gangs and participate in subcultures as a result of **status frustration** – they see few legitimate opportunities for upward mobility towards success and society's rewards, as the Chicago School and strain theory suggested in the previous chapter. Subcultures then become spaces for disadvantaged youth (or, presumably, older people as well) to come together and to celebrate their deviant characteristics. Skinheads provide the classic example. Economically marginalized with little hope for a better future, they nevertheless glorify their working-class roots, making toughness, aggression, and manual labor the hallmarks of "real" manhood.

From the outset, scholars and authorities associated subcultures with crime. In fact, in some contexts subcultural affiliation automatically garners the attention of law enforcement, as in the case of Juggalos in the US, punks in Indonesia, or gopniks in Russia (more on this in Chapter 6). Some subcultures, such as graffiti-writing, do revolve around what is technically criminal activity. Others, such as soccer hooligans and "ultras," regularly engage in violence. Certainly drugs and alcohol play a large role in many (both youth and adult) lives, but there is no denying their special significance in certain scenes such as hippie and rave. Mods took copious amounts of Quaaludes, and so did disco freaks. So perhaps people are drawn to subcultures in order to engage in crime. Subcultures may teach the *techniques* of crime (e.g. how to con someone) as well as offering a justification, or rationalization, for criminal activity (Sutherland and Cressey 1978).

Despite these important insights, views of subcultures as criminal enterprises or products of social disorganization are flawed in several respects. First, while it is certainly true that subcultures may be particularly attractive to people already socially marginalized (e.g. working-class youth), people from stable communities and in supportive, "normative" families still find joy and meaning in subcultural participation. Subcultures are more than simply reactions to larger structural forces. Second, subculturists may be *deviant*, but they are not always *delinquent* or criminal. Authorities connect subcultures too closely to delinquency and crime despite the fact that many subculturists are basically law-abiding. Subcultures may share characteristics with gangs, may even overlap with gangs, but as I explained in Chapter 1 they differ in significant ways. Finally, these sorts of explanations suggest that subcultural participation is abnormal, an aberration, a product of dysfunctional relationships and a disorganized society. I will emphasize throughout this book that subculturists, while deviant, are typically not the folk devils that inhabit reformers' imaginations. Similarly, casting subcultures as havens for anti-social delinquents reinforces the dubious notion that "mainstream" society is automatically good/functional/beneficial/better or even that a "normal" society exists in the first place.

DISTINCTION: DO PEOPLE JUST WANT TO BE DIFFERENT?

Many of us can probably recall a time where we wanted to stand out from the crowd, perhaps even remembering the strategies we used to show just how "different" we were. Most people want at once to feel accepted and part of a community while also feeling different; the focus on individualistic expression is especially prevalent, even *pushed*, in contemporary Western societies. Given the individualization associated with modernity that I discussed earlier, it comes as little surprise that people might identify with subcultures to feel unique when in fact in most significant ways we are not. Just as importantly, subcultures help define who we are *not*. In his classic book *Distinction*, Pierre Bourdieu (1984) shows how people of different social classes distinguish themselves from one another. The upper classes create an aesthetic different from and largely unavailable to others, amassing **cultural capital** such as designer clothes and expensive jewelry, but also titles, activities, and ways of speaking. While this sort of distinction reinforces class hierarchies, subculturists also seek distinction, cultivating **subcultural capital** in the form of tattoos, records, and insider knowledge (Thornton 1995). Subcultures may also reflect a basic desire to be different from another "class" of people, often constructed as "the mainstream." At times, outsiders may find subculturists' efforts at distinction tedious and self-absorbed, or even narcissistic desires to "get attention." I would argue that rather than reflecting some personal flaw, the desire of some subculturists to stand out reflects the broader social imperative of modernity to carefully craft a desirable self – albeit in sometimes a more spectacular fashion!

LEISURE SPACES: SUBCULTURISTS JUST WANT TO HAVE FUN?

One of the simplest explanations for why people participate in subcultures is also among the best: perhaps people participate in subcultures to enjoy themselves, whether by listening to music or skateboarding. Recall from Chapter 1 that the **clubculture** and **post-subculture** theories suggest just that, claiming that diffuse scenes come together to have a good time, absent much of an overt political agenda. The "Soulies" of England's Northern Soul scene loved dancing to their beloved American soul artists while using amphetamines (Wilson 2007). Traceurs – practitioners of the urban gymnastics known as parkour – find joy in leaping across cityscapes (Kidder 2012). Riot grrrls have fun making music and printing 'zines, and ravers find ecstasy-fueled bliss dancing to electronic dance music. Subcultures, then, are leisure spaces.

While leisure certainly plays a significant role in subcultures, the contemporary world offers many ways to have fun. The question remains why people pursue *subcultural* leisure, which often carries greater social (and sometimes physical) risks than participating in sports, social clubs, or more conventional hobbies. It seems as if people seek ever new, more extreme ways of having fun and expressing themselves. One does not tattoo one's face simply for fun, nor does one casually leap from the top of one building to another. While daily survival remains a struggle for much of the world's population, there are many who live increasingly predictable, routine, mundane, even "safe" lives. Perhaps certain subcultures respond to the *predictability*, even the *boredom* of contemporary life? **Edgework** describes "a clearly observable threat to one's physical or mental well-being or one's sense of an ordered existence," undertaken voluntarily (Lyng 1990: 857), that provides the opportunity for "creative, skilful, self-determining action" (Lyng 1990: 877). Institutions increasingly regulate, monitor, even constrain our lives, resulting in alienation and a feeling of lacking control over one's life. Some people crave the freedom and sense of control found in exploring the boundaries between order and disorder, normality and deviance. Subcultures with a high degree of bodily risk – bike messengers, parkour, roller derby, BASE jumping – clearly illustrate edgework, involving an embodied excitement, a rush that comes from using one's skills to overcome challenges, from being so in the moment that the rest of the world fades into the background (Kidder 2006). Not as obvious may be the risks associated with less physically dangerous deviant identities and practices such as burlesque and goth. Yet many subculturists willingly take on risks of judgment or even ostracism and violence, as they stretch the boundaries between acceptance and stigma. Why, you may wonder, would someone tattoo her face, presumably knowing the difficulties face tattoos might pose to getting a job? While psychological explanations may be tempting – she is disturbed or was abused – we might also see such body modification as rational edgework. Willingly stepping outside social norms can provide a sort of "rush," a sense of satisfaction unavailable via more conventional avenues.

SUBCULTURES AS STRATEGIES?

The vast variety of subcultures makes explaining their emergence in one neat and tidy theory nearly impossible. And the great diversity of subculturists poses a challenge to finding a perfect theory of participation. At a minimum, we can examine subcultures as **strategies** participants use to respond to their social surroundings and tackle everyday concerns and problems. Such an approach encompasses many of the points I make in this chapter. If our "self" is a project and a performance, a work in progress, then subcultures become ideal strategies for crafting identities, achieving distinction, and having fun. Subculturists are not necessarily alienated or marginalized, although they may be. Subculturists do not simply or automatically respond to structural changes and social problems such as modernization in predictable, predetermined ways. Rather, they bring a degree of agency and creativity to their participation. Rather than focusing on subcultures as relatively homogenous class- and style-based groupings (à la the CCCS) or fluid consumption-based scenes (post-subculturists), our focus should turn to the *substance* of such groupings (Pilkington and Omel'chenko 2013). What do participants *do*, and what do they think about what they do?

Most importantly, and perhaps contrary to conventional wisdom, subcultural participation is, by and large, *rational*, that is, reasoned and intentional. Subcultures offer strategies to overcome the meaninglessness of post/modernity. They enable subculturists to join with likeminded others to carve out "safe," affirming spaces in which they can find solidarity and share their interests. Subcultures can be strategic places for people to experiment with identities not necessarily accepted in other contexts. Finally, subcultures may be strategies to explore and express discontent with the parent culture, government and other authorities, more typical peers, and even other subcultures (more on this in Chapters 3 and 4).

KEY INSIGHTS

- The explosion of subcultures over the last century reflects a plethora of changes associated with industrialization, modernity, and globalization. Especially relevant are the rise of consumer culture, the unmooring of identity, the creation of "youth" as a life stage, and the expansion of media access.
- There is no evidence that subculturists, broadly speaking, are more apt to have psychological or emotional problems than other, more conventional, groups. Put simply, people do not participate in "strange" subcultures simply because they themselves are strange. However, it's likely that the stigma and potential harassment subculturists face may *contribute to* depression and other problems.
- Participation in and identification with subcultures is fairly rational. Subcultures meet individuals' social needs, provide leisure spaces, and form "safe" places for people who fall outside the norm.
- Subcultural participation also provides strategies to experiment with identities, connect with likeminded people, and explore "taboo" subjects and activities.

EXPLORING FURTHER

Wannabes, Goths, and Christians: The Boundaries of Sex, Style, and Status, by Amy C. Wilkins, 2008 (University of Chicago Press). Ethnographic study comparing and contrasting the gender, sexual, class, and racial strategies of goths, Christians, and white girl "wannabes."

Sells Like Teen Spirit: Music, Youth Culture, and Social Crisis, by Ryan Moore, 2010 (New York University Press). Explores how the economic, political, and cultural changes of the twentieth century produced the punk, metal, alternative/grunge, riot grrrl, retro and other music scenes.

Northern Soul, directed by Elaine Constantine, 2013. A feature film depicting the British Northern Soul scene at its peak in the 1970s. Enchanted by underground American soul music, "Soulies" cultivated a unique dance style, fashion sense, and club scene that remains influential today.

My Playground, directed by Kaspar Astrup Schröder. Documentary explaining how parkour transforms urban spaces, breathing life into otherwise disenchanted spaces. Features freerunners from Denmark, Japan, China, and the US and UK. http://release.kasparworks.com

Dream World, directed by Frank Sauer, 2012. A short film capturing the freedom, friendship, and fulfillment experienced by several freerunners. Available at Vimeo.com.

3

HOW DO SUBCULTURES RESIST "MAINSTREAM" SOCIETY ... AND ARE THEY SUCCESSFUL?

In early 2012, former Russian President Vladimir Putin was poised to retake the presidency amid accusations of election fraud and abuse of power. Protestors crowded city streets calling for fair elections and other reforms, chanting "Russia without Putin!" and demanding freedom for political prisoners. Having been appointed Prime Minister by his successor, Dmitry Medvedev, Putin's election, which he eventually won, would add at least four more years to his already 12 years in power. Amid the discontent, a feminist punk collective known as Pussy Riot staged several illegal protest events, clad in brightly colored dresses and tights, faces masked by matching balaclavas. Members of the collective, who remain anonymous, had earlier orchestrated protests in subways and outside a prison where authorities held an opposition leader, filming and posting their actions on YouTube. Moscow authorities arrested, detained, and fined the women for performing an anti-Putin song titled "Putin Pissed Himself" in snowy Red Square (Flintoff 2012). In March, the collective offered a punk rock "prayer" for Putin's removal, playing "Virgin Mary, Mother of God, Expel Putin!" at the altar in the Cathedral of Christ the Savior. Convicted of hooliganism, a Moscow judge sentenced two women to two years in a penal colony with a reputation for harsh treatment. While some members of the Orthodox church pled for leniency, the church

Patriarch called the band's actions sacrilegious, claiming "the devil laughed at us" (Elder 2012).

Inspired by the feminist politics and DIY creativity of the 1990s riot grrrl movement in the US, Pussy Riot carries on a long tradition of subculturists who challenge the status quo. Yet not all subculturists engage in politics, commit civil disobedience, or even actively seek to challenge authority; in some ways, Pussy Riot is the exception, not the rule. Still, most subculturists profess some sort of resistance to the "mainstream." Whether any sort of coherent "mainstream" exists is beside the point; subculturists construct a vision of an oppressive/conformist/boring culture to which they contrast themselves. In this chapter, I consider subcultures' potential to offer meaningful resistance to the status quo. Put bluntly, do subcultures simply offer spaces for kids to listen to music, play dress-up, and maybe occasionally shock their elders or do they challenge society in some meaningful way? Are subculturists truly rebellious or rebels without a cause?

WHAT *IS* RESISTANCE – WHAT *COUNTS*?

When we think of significant, intentional efforts to change the world we often look to social movements. An example might be environmental group Greenpeace organizing a public demonstration in Japan against whaling practices, demanding that government officials create or enforce conservation policies. Similarly, Occupy activists protest global inequality by taking over public spaces from New York to Sydney. Often led by charismatic leaders such as Mahatma Gandhi, Nelson Mandela, Wangari Maathai, or Martin Luther King, Jr., social movements seem to be everything subcultures are not: organized, externally focused, collective, and political. In contrast, subcultures might seem diffuse, self-centered, individualistic opportunities for personal expression, thus marking movements as serious contenders for social change and subcultures as trivial in comparison. "Real" efforts towards change, or "real" resistance to power, then, equals professional social movement organizations and activists organizing public protest campaigns.

Despite this grim portrayal of the prospects of subcultural defiance, the dichotomy between leisure and politics misses important, but less visible, acts of resistance. Power is a social relationship wherein one party influences or compels another to think, act, or feel in a certain way. Power relations exist between nations, governments and their people, corporations and their consumers and so forth, but they also exist among smaller groups and individuals. At the most basic level, subculturists often attempt to subvert inequalities of power by challenging dominant social ideas and practices. Punks' outlandish hairstyles, obnoxious music, panhandling, and anarchy patches initially shocked more conventional standards of beauty, art, productive work, and social order. Subculturists undermine the **hegemonic**, or dominant, social meanings and power relationships that in many ways govern our lives. Hegemony can be both political and cultural (Gramsci 1971). Politicians (and other power brokers) such as Vladimir Putin seem to have a monopoly on political power, especially the legitimate use of violence. But power wielded at the barrel of a gun can be expensive and messy; *cultural* (or ideological) hegemony makes power seem invisible. The ultimate expression of hegemony occurs when people come to believe and enforce the ideas of the powerful, in effect doing the "work" of the powerful for them. For example, some poor or working-class people oppose tax increases on the rich because they are convinced people get their just rewards – rich people are smart, have worked hard, and thus *deserve* their wealth, while poor folk must be irresponsible, less capable, or less hardworking. Likewise, women often reinforce sexist, patriarchal culture by holding one another to impossible beauty standards; they have absorbed the rules of the gender "game." Both of these examples illustrate how ideology legitimates the privilege and power of one group over another. So in some sense, countering hegemonic ideas (or *frames*) perpetuated by powerful people and institutions is a significant act of resistance.

In thinking about what "counts" as resistance, we might begin with wondering how subcultures disrupt or counter hegemony. This means that meaningful resistance does not always have to be *revolutionary*, in the sense of radically altering the social order. Resistance is not always directed towards the state, nor does it always take the form of public protest. While sometimes quite direct, subcultural resistance is often more subtle than political protest. In any case, we are interested in not only what subculturists *think* but (perhaps more importantly) in what they *do*.

BIRMINGHAM SCHOOL: IS RESISTANCE ILLUSORY?

Resistance as a theoretical concept gained popularity with the CCCS/Birmingham School. Scholars in this tradition saw subculturists as more than delinquent kids. Working class youth, especially, resisted conformist, hegemonic culture through their style and rituals (Hall and Jefferson 1976). Mods, rockers, skinheads, and especially punks shocked adults with their spectacular fashions, obnoxious music, and rowdy behavior. Their **style** (for example, skinheads' shaved heads, boots, and braces) and their **rituals** (such as punks' slam dancing) symbolized their rejection of middle-class, bourgeois lifestyles. In a sense, working-class subcultural youth were **semiotic warriors**, meaning they challenged the status quo through their signs or symbols. Denied a legitimate chance at well-paid jobs, disadvantaged youth fought back with the only resources at their disposal, their style, leisure, and consumptive practices. However, according to the CCCS, such resistance was largely "magical," or illusory, changing little and often reinforcing the very status hierarchies they presumably sought to undermine. Resistance rarely, if ever, led to better access to education, healthcare, good salaries, and so on. Thus skinheads, in championing working-class identity and jobs further ensured their exploitation (see Willis 1977). Such views likely echo popular conceptions of subcultures as mildly subversive, but ultimately leisure-oriented spaces where kids drink, smoke, have sex, listen to music, and occasionally commit petty crimes.

Some critique the CCCS for portraying working class youth as making a heroic (if ineffectual) stand against an oppressive hegemonic culture – casting subculturists as heroes and adult culture as monolithic are both empirically suspect. Furthermore, not all subculturists are young, working class men responding to inequality. Alternately, the CCCS is perhaps too pessimistic in suggesting that youth resistance was ultimately illusory, due in part to the overemphasis on class struggle – there are more ways to make change than challenging economic forces.

POST-SUBCULTURE: KIDS JUST WANT TO HAVE FUN?

Regarding the first critique of the CCCS, **post-subculture theorists** have been critical of the entire notion of resistance, focusing even more on the consumerist aspects of youth culture. David Muggleton and Rupert Weinzierl (2003) acknowledge the political/cultural significance of youth while cautioning against reinforcing a "heroic" image of subcultural youth. After all, subcultural youth such as those present in the rave scene would rather do drugs and dance than change the world – or so the thinking goes. Thus Ted Polhemus (1998) suggests youth cultures may be hedonistic, apolitical, consumerist escapes, youth focused more on identity shopping and personal fulfillment than social resistance. Indeed, at first glance a large part of subcultural experience is consuming items given particular subcultural meanings – a rave DJ purchases a rare record, a Kustom Kar aficionado buys expensive rims for his hot rod, or an Otaku obsessively collects manga, anime, and video games. Muggleton (1997: 200) suggests that post-subculturists emphasize "the surface qualities of the spectacle at the expense of any underlying ideologies of resistance." What's more, perhaps the more conventional public have simply become accustomed to all manner of weird groups and strange lifestyles. Steve Redhead (1990) is critical of the meta-narrative of the "liberation of youth," claiming that subcultures have lost their shock value in the post-punk world, often reflecting the mainstream or a nostalgia for the past. Rather than offering meaningful resistance, contemporary subcultures seek to reincarnate – through their consumption – a mythical era of "authentic" subcultures. The number of 16-year-olds sporting t-shirts from 1970s bands such as Black Sabbath, the Ramones, the Sex Pistols, and the Misfits may bolster this argument. In any case, subcultures focus more inwardly, are perhaps more self-absorbed than engaged in meaningful social criticism. Sarah Thornton (1995) suggests that internal subcultural politics of authenticity and a focus on difference simply create new hierarchies reflective of those present in the mainstream world subcultures propose to defy – similar to the CCCS analysis of resistance, but without even the intimation of social resistance. Finally, while acknowledging "neo-tribes" as spaces providing "sovereignty over one's own existence," Maffesoli (1996: 42, 51) also worries that the "festive dimension" of neo-tribal resistance is oriented "less at changing the world than getting used to and tinkering with it." Even more critically, Joseph Heath and Andrew Potter (2004: 6) argue that "countercultural rebellion has reinvigorated consumer capitalism" and detracted from the more effective reform efforts of social movements:

> Having fun is not subversive, and it doesn't undermine any system. In fact, widespread hedonism makes it more difficult to organize social movements, and much more difficult to persuade anyone to make a sacrifice in the name of social justice.

IT'S COMPLICATED: HOW DO SUBCULTURES SIMULTANEOUSLY CHALLENGE AND REINFORCE DOMINANT SOCIAL IDEAS AND RELATIONS?

So the CCCS may have exaggerated subculturists' focus on resistance, engaging in a bit of wishful thinking. And post-subculture theorists rightly point out that many subculturists focus more on partying and having a good time than on politics. But does that mean resistance is futile?

Contemporary scholars have thought about resistance in new ways, acknowledging the post-subculture critiques of the Birmingham School while examining resistance from subculturists' point of view. Laurain Leblanc (1999) in her study of women punks asserts that participants' subjective understanding of their involvement reveals a more nuanced understanding of resistance. She found that punk girls recognized the sexism in the punk scene, but still found meaning in consciously defying the "femininity game," dominant standards of feminine beauty and manners. They might not always be challenging the structural disadvantages women face (such as wage discrimination), but these punk women still found personal empowerment in their resistance.

My own work on straight edge (Haenfler 2004b) demonstrates there are different **meanings** (individual and collective), **sites** (micro, meso, and macro), **and methods** (personal and political) **of resistance**. Most straight edgers experience intensely personal meaning in abstaining from alcohol and tobacco; for some, the identity is part of a personal quest to deal with past addiction or to reject an abusive family history. Yet most also see straight edge as a collective challenge to cultural norms of excess, a "brotherhood" of shared values. Resistance is also contextual, occurring in a variety of sites. At the micro level, straight edgers might challenge abuse at home and conformity at school. At the meso level, they seek to challenge a perceived intoxicated youth culture, including other youth *subcultures* such as punk; often subcultural youth are resisting/challenging *other youth* as much as they are thinking of the larger "adult" society. And at the macro level, straight edgers resist the largely unquestioned assumption that alcohol be part of most social situations, suggesting even that drugs and alcohol constitute one way to pacify people into larger patterns of conformity. Finally, straight edgers employed both personal and political methods of resistance. As I've suggested, subcultures often offer a less overt challenge to power than do social movements. Straight edgers typically seek to lead by personal example, living out the values they profess by (often literally) wearing their politics on their sleeves. Anyone can refuse drugs and alcohol. What sets straight edgers apart is their emphasis on public display of drug-free living, their professed lifetime commitment, and their crafting of an identity around abstinence. These practices symbolize for many a greater, more political rejection of mainstream culture, leading some straight edgers to vegetarianism, anti-fascism, anti-sexism, peace, environmental, and other causes (see Kuhn 2010). Many straight edgers self-consciously understand that their *personal* resistance is part of a greater *political* challenge (Haenfler 2006).

J. Patrick Williams (2009, 2011) further consolidates the new thinking about resistance, discussing three **dimensions of resistance**, each existing on a continuum. First, he notes that resistance can be relatively *passive* or *active*, based upon subculturists' *intention* to resist. As I discussed above, the CCCS largely viewed subculturists' efforts as passive – youth were *consuming* deviant fashions, twisting dominant styles to their own purposes, but were doing little to challenge the social class structure or to really improve their lot in life. However, as the more contemporary ethnographic studies I discuss here have shown, subculturists (such as Leblanc's punk women) regularly report more active, thoughtful, and intentional efforts at change, in turn challenging some of the post-subculturists' view of youth scenes as apolitical, hedonistic escapes. That doesn't mean they always get the results they seek, nor does it mean we must judge their resistance as effective (effects are difficult to measure anyway). Recognizing subculturists' motivations behind and interpretations of their actions does suggest we take subcultural resistance seriously, if not uncritically.

Second, active resistance can occur between the *micro* and *macro* levels, based upon subculturists' "targets." Again, attention to subculturists' subjective understandings and lived experiences is crucial. At the micro level, Mexican "emo" kids may adopt the emo/goth style and identity as a sort of social psychological self-defense against the popular kids who torment them. At the meso level, they may challenge the gender norms in local youth scenes or "jock" culture at their schools, while at the macro level they call attention to government corruption or drug violence. Likewise on the more macro end of the continuum, African hip hoppers use their music to critique the excesses of globalization (Ntarangwi 2009), just as the 60s counterculture offered a (relatively) comprehensive critique of the dominant culture *and* an alternative way of life.

Third, resistance can be *overt* and/or *covert*, based upon whether subculturists intend for their actions to be interpreted as resistance and if outsiders *do* in fact recognize resistance as such (see Hollander and Einwohner 2004). Overt resistance is typically easy to spot – a long-haired black metal guy wearing an inverted cross and a "Fuck Me Jesus" t-shirt while walking down a main thoroughfare in Stockholm isn't exactly being subtle. A crust punk running her own "distro" (a small-scale, DIY distribution outlet for underground records, 'zines, and other subcultural paraphernalia) at a show in defiance of capitalism engages in a more covert form of resistance. Her efforts likely go unnoticed by outsiders. Even while critical of dominant institutions, some subcultural activity is meant primarily for insiders. Yet resistance can be both covert and overt; Japanese subcultures serve, in part, as resistance to the archetypical rule-following, conformist "salary man" who works exhausting hours at a dull job, unquestioningly devoted to his work. Their subcultural activities may often be inward-directed, but outsiders recognize their pursuit of creative and expressive activities as a real alternative to the corporate grind.

HEAVY METAL MUSLIMS

Heavy metal, punk, and hip hop have a strong presence across the Muslim world, from Morocco and Pakistan to Palestine and Indonesia. In some of these contexts, professing subcultural/counter-hegemonic ideas is especially subversive. When women rap in

Morocco or Indonesian metal bands criticize Islamist authorities, they take a significant risk and often provoke a harsh response. It would be hard to argue that such resistance is totally "illusory."

Returning to the question of whether or not subcultures end up resisting or reinforcing dominant power relations, a number of scholars have done interesting work on the *complexity* of resistance. Both Dunja Brill (2008) and Amy Wilkins' (2004) studies of goths showed that the scene provides women a space to reject "passive" femininity and engage in "active sexuality" as well as opportunities for men to enact more androgynous gender displays. Yet Wilkins notes the compulsion for women to dress sexily and be sexually available for men, while Brill writes of a "cult of femininity" for both sexes that in many ways preserves dominant gender ideologies and practices as men are given more room for gender play. Similarly, my own work on straight edge revealed two contradictory faces of straight edge masculinity. The progressive, or self-styled "positive" face encouraged youth to reject many of the markers of young manhood such as drinking and sexual conquest, even homophobia, violence, and eating meat. The so-called "militant" branch of the scene encouraged hypermasculine behavior, creating judgmental, violent thugs. Finally, while many have noted the hedonism and drug use in rave cultures, Angela McRobbie (2000) interpreted raves as symbolic, pleasurable escape from the mundane. Brian Wilson (2002) notes that many participants in Canadian raves translated the PLUR ethos – peace, love, unity, and respect – into their daily lives outside rave parties, suggesting that some ravers saw their activities as "tactical resistance."

All of this is to say that scholars are finding ways to think about resistance that neither inappropriately cast youth as heroic cultural revolutionaries nor reduce participants' experiences to ineffectual consumerism. Williams (2011: 94) writes, "examples or moments of resistance cannot easily be placed into boxes" and that "subcultural youths have the ability to act within their everyday environments, even in the face of limited resources and ideological hegemony." Resistance, unsurprisingly, is not all or nothing – youth cultures both resist *and* reinforce dominate social relations and inequalities.

POLITICS AND SOCIAL MOVEMENTS: HOW DO SUBCULTURISTS ENGAGE DIRECTLY IN SOCIAL CHANGE?

As I discussed near the beginning of this chapter, subcultures can seem like relatively trivial, escapist fashion shows, leaving "real" change to protesters and politicians. However, some subculturists take on active, overt resistance against meso and macro level targets, fusing their subcultural identities with direct efforts at change. They pursue social change in a variety of ways such as supporting charities and nonprofits, participating in protest movements, and even entering the political arena. For instance, hip hoppers have been involved in registering people to vote, skateboarders raise money for underprivileged kids, and anarchist subcultures have utilized the "black bloc" tactic in anti-globalization and other protests around the world.

CHARITIES AND NONPROFITS

Rather than fitting the stereotypical image of anti-social misfits or disorganized hellraisers, some subculturists undertake distinctly *pro-social* activities, volunteering their time or raising money in support of charitable causes. Straight edge hardcore band Have Heart is one of many hardcore bands that have raised funds for women's shelters and other nonprofit organizations. The Patriot Guard Riders are motorcycle aficionados who attend (at the family's invitation) funerals for military personal, firefighters, and police officers, sheltering the grieving family from protest groups such as the anti-gay Westboro Baptist Church, known for picketing soldiers' funerals, claiming their deaths are God's retribution for cultural immorality. Cosplayers – participants in a fandom who enjoy creating and wearing costumes – often visit children's hospitals or collect money for schools. Such work not only provides a social benefit but also legitimates subculturists' "deviant" behavior; dressing up as Mr. Spock or Darth Vader seems less strange when done to entertain sick children. Skateboarders harassed for skating in urban areas shine up their public image by raising money for a skate park.

PREFIGURATIVE POLITICS AND LIFESTYLE MOVEMENTS

Some subculturists forge political identities in the midst of their involvement, making subcultures a form of prefigurative politics. **Prefigurative politics** include activists' efforts to live out the more ideal world they envision, laying the cultural and/or tactical groundwork for an eventual challenge to the government or other power structures (Breines 1989). Thus movements such as anarchism that seek to undermine hierarchies of all kinds organize their groups around consensus decision-making or participatory democracy. Anti-capitalist punks circumvent capitalism as much as possible as they create their own DIY music and art. White power movements have long used punk and skinhead subcultures as recruiting grounds, turning Nazi skinheads into race warriors (Blazak 2001). The 1989 solidarity movements in Central Europe built upon informal youth networks, including underground punk, that paved the way for more direct political confrontation (Kenney 2003). Thus subcultures can help sow and nurture seeds of discontent that eventually grow into political dissent. In apartheid-era South Africa, youth rocked the status quo by forming multi-racial punk and reggae bands (e.g. National Wake) while integrated UK ska acts such as Madness and The Specials promoted unity and respect (Jones and Maas 2012). While not necessarily engaging *directly* in anti-racist politics (e.g. street protests, petitions), the mere presence of multi-racial bands made a powerful social statement that contributed to the ongoing shift in race relations, *prefiguring* a different future. Riot grrrl "zinesters" view their 'zine-making as both personal empowerment and political challenge. Grrrls use 'zines as opportunities to express ideas that would elsewhere be marginalized, resisting, in the lyrics of riot grrrl band Bikini Kill (1994), "psychic death." But 'zines also serve as "border spaces" where women can practice participatory democracy, build alliances, and organize around feminist and queer issues (Schilt and Zobl 2008).

Relatedly, subcultures often overlap with **lifestyle movements**, "loosely bound collectivities in which participants advocate lifestyle change as a primary means to social change, politicizing daily life while pursuing morally coherent 'authentic' identities" (Haenfler et al. 2012: 14). Less organized than traditional social movements, lifestyle movements encourage individuals to make changes in their everyday lives in an effort to enact cultural change. Many straight edgers not only abstain from alcohol but also adopt *and promote* vegetarian or vegan lifestyles, believing that their individual efforts collectively make a difference. Riley, Griffin, and Morey (2010) argue that even seemingly hedonistic electronic dance music fans engage in "everyday politics"; *not* engaging with official political institutions constitutes an "active aloofness" that denies legitimacy to power structures while creating communities where participants can live out alternative values. Likewise, anarchist subcultures see anti-consumption as tactical resistance even as they use it to express their anarchist identity, bond with likeminded others, and distinguish themselves from typical consumers. They refuse many of the goods associated with middle-class life – a stable home, a car, stylish clothes, meat, even beauty and body-care products – as part of a larger rejection of oppressive and environmentally destructive industries (Portwood-Stacer 2012). Subcultures often align with lifestyle movements, as both combine expressive identities, cultural challenge, and personal and social transformation. Lifestyle movements and their subcultural participants can even serve as "**collective action reservoirs**," that is pools of likeminded people not regularly politically active who may be mobilized for a particular protest action or political campaign (Haenfler et al. 2012); both the global democracy and Occupy movements drew punks and other subculturists into their struggle (Ruggero 2012).

POSITIVE FORCE DC

Since the 1980s, Positive Force DC has been "an activist collective seeking radical social change, personal growth, and youth empowerment." Forged in the early hardcore punk scene, the organization stages benefit concerts, art shows, and film screenings, as well as working directly with disadvantaged people (such as homeless women) in the Washington, DC, area. Members played an active role in the anti-apartheid movement, forming annoying "punk percussion protests" that drummed incessantly outside the South African embassy.

www.positiveforcedc.org

SOCIAL MOVEMENTS

Some subculturists engage directly in what we more traditionally think of as social movements. Punks, for example, used their DIY independent media to help mobilize participants in the Rock Against Racism movement in the UK and the peace movement in the US (Roberts and Moore 2009; Goddyer 2003). Punk music and culture actually shaped these movements' tactics and messages, becoming a "mobilizing structure" that helped protestors organize. DIY ideology and, more importantly, DIY *skills* provided punks the means to mobilize support; punk shows and 'zines were forums to build anti-racist and peace activism. And of course music has long been a staple of protest movements, from the folk rock of the 60s to hip hop today (see Eyerman and Jamison 1998).

How do subcultures and movements interact? First, as I discussed above, subcultures can act as prefigurative politics, even **free spaces**, places relatively removed from (and safe from the surveillance of) dominant groups in which activists can build collective identity and even develop tactics (Goodwin and Jasper 2009). Free spaces can be actual places (e.g. churches in the Civil Rights movement, prisons in apartheid-era South Africa), but can also be subcultural communities. Authorities by and large likely do not see fixed gear bicyclists as political, but communities of DIY cyclists develop "bike activism" in events such as Critical Mass rides to resist car culture (Furness 2010). Subcultures act as **submerged networks** (Melucci 1989) "in which experiments in life are carried on, new experiences created, and collective identities forged in everyday life" (Nash 2010: 113). For instance, BD/SM, polyamory, and other sexual subcultures may help nurture a queer collective identity and counter-hegemonic political ideology even while existing primarily for leisure and friendship. Similarly to being potential collective action reservoirs, subcultures may also serve as **abeyance structures**, networks in which activists keep a movement alive through an unfavorable political climate, ensuring movement continuity even when the situation seems bleak (Taylor 1989). Protest movements typically occur in waves, or cycles of protest, including moments of significant activity and momentum and times of "abeyance" when activity wanes. The US women's movement has included several waves of protest where participation and activism peaks and declines. Between such cycles, when commentators often declare feminism "dead," women keep feminism alive in music festivals, feminist/queer bookstores, 'zines, blogs, and other media, and yes, subcultures. The combination of deeply-held (often deviant) values with leisure and friendship networks helps some subcultures effectively play all of these roles in social movements.

Acting as free spaces, submerged networks, and abeyance structures in which dissident ideas and practices can ferment, subculturists become potential constituencies ripe for mobilization. Some social movement leaders see subcultures as fertile recruiting grounds. Tom Metzger, founder of White Aryan Resistance in the US, coopted a variety of youth music scenes into his movement, including skinheads, punks, and metalheads (Moore 1993; Burghart 1999). Racist movements have long used white power music to bolster their cause. Ugo Corte and Bob Edwards (2008: 7) report that especially prior to the spread of the internet, "White Power music played an integral role in spreading and internationalizing a highly fragmented racist movement" across Western Europe and North America, as touring bands, record labels, and 'zines gave some sense of coherence to disparate scenes. Racist movements used music subcultures to recruit new adherents, foster a common (collective) identity, and raise money. People who might not otherwise be interested in traditional politics or protest may appreciate the emotional pull of music and the camaraderie of a subculture. In the process, they come into contact with movement activists and ideologies in the context of a meaningful community, potentially adopting aspects of a movement's worldview.

Each of these connections between subcultures and movements foster **oppositional identities** and **shared meanings**. Straight edge kids around the world connect their straight edge identity to social change. Dutch straight edge band Manliftingbanner promoted communist and anti-fascist politics with hardcore music throughout the 1990s. Similarly, Sweden's Refused incorporated radical social critique into their hardcore and straight edge identities, including manifestos with their records addressing topics as varied as alienation, media domination, corporate imperialism, and MTV. Believing in the revolutionary potential of music, they wrote, "The art produced by Refused is a weapon in the service of the struggle and an inseparable part of it" (Refused n.d.). Some straight edgers engage in nonviolent direct action campaigns. Israeli anarchist Jonathan Pollak cofounded Anarchists Against the Wall, an activist collective that, among other things, works in solidarity with Palestinian organizations. Arrested many times and severely injured in demonstrations against the West Bank barrier, he explains how his subcultural and activist passions intersect (Kuhn 2010: 112):

> The need to extract oneself from society, so prevalent in Straight Edge, is fuelled by the desire to see and live a different reality; a desire that can't subsist in the clubs, cafes and drug culture of mainstream society. Both my Straight Edge and my activism are strongly rooted in this passion ...

Because they often serve as such important sources of meaning and identity, subcultures offer a variety of resources (e.g. music, 'zines, websites) with which to "**frame**" issues, that is to intentionally communicate and shape the meanings surrounding a group of people, a set of circumstances, or an event (see Snow et al. 1986). So progressive punks might frame capitalism as oppressive and dehumanizing; straight edge kids frame alcohol as a poison used by those in power to pacify those they exploit; and White Power subcultures frame immigrants as criminals and invaders that "pollute" the white race. Subcultures, then, can serve as a cultural resource mobilized by social movements across the political spectrum.

Egyptian rappers Arabian Knightz song "Not Your Prisoner" framed the Mubarak regime and others like it as unjust, oppressive, even evil, fueling and capturing the spirit of the revolution during the January 2011 revolt. Rapper El Général's arrest resulting from his song critical of Tunisian President Ben Ali played some role in the Tunisian revolution and in turn transformed hip hop from a music supposedly for thugs and gangsters into a cultural sensation (Ulysses 2012). And just as subculturists may help inspire uprisings, so to do social movements inspire scenes; the Arab uprisings fueled new political consciousness in Libyan, Egyptian, and Tunisian hip hop, for example. While the complete role of hip hop in the uprisings remains unclear (and outsiders should avoid transposing their own hopes onto the scene), the connections between hip hop and protest around the world are real.

POLITICS: CAN SUBCULTURES BE A POLITICAL FORCE?

At times, subculturists participate in more conventional politics, trying to influence elections or using subcultural capital to mobilize efforts to change policy. The Rock Against Racism campaign in the UK inspired US punks to Rock Against Reagan in the early 1980s (see Mattson 2001). In 2004, "Fat Mike" of punk label Fat Wreck Chords and band NOFX spearheaded a Rock Against Bush campaign to oppose the re-election of George W. Bush. Using concerts, compilation records, and a web site (PunkVoter), prominent punk bands raised more than $1 million for voter registration drives as well as spreading a pro-peace/anti-Bush message. Australian punks did likewise, organizing in opposition to Prime Minister John Howard. Racist, anti-immigrant rightwing parties such as Italy's Forza Nuova, Germany's New Democratic Party, and Sweden's New Democracy have not only capitalized on the prefigurative and social movement activities of White Power subcultures but have even incorporated such groups into their recruitment campaigns (Corte and Edwards 2008).

SUBCULTURAL SPACES AS "WAKER CELLS"

Even as subcultures "are increasingly experienced through capitalist and internet mediations," subcultural spaces can serve as "waker cells," semi-autonomous and often temporary places where participants can "plot spontaneity, life, communalism, anarchism, and autonomy" (Clark 2004: 453, 454). For example, anarchist squats, clubs, and coffee houses provide places for subculturists to practice their ideals (prefigurative politics) and plot political resistance. Dylan Clark (2004) describes the Black Cat Café – a cooperatively owned and run restaurant in 1990's Seattle populated primarily by anarchopunks – as an imminently political space. Its exterior – painted black and marked by the anarchist black cat – shielded an interior covered with radical posters and flyers for punk shows. Leftist books and pamphlets provided ample reading material and patrons argued politics as they enjoyed the vegetarian menu. While the café eventually closed, many regulars joined in the "Battle of Seattle" street demonstrations of 1999, a significant moment in the global justice movement.

Subculturists rally periodically for a variety of causes. In the UK, subculturists rallied against the Criminal Justice and Public Order Act of 1994 which increased restrictions and penalties on "alternative" cultures such as rave, squatting, and new age travelers as well as political activities such as fox hunt disruptions (McKay 1996). The "anti-globalization" movement, known for massive protests between 1999 and 2003 in places such as Seattle, Quebec, London, Genoa, and Athens, brought together a variety of protesters, including many subculturists. While lacking clear leadership and organization, this "movement of movements" demonstrated that "subcultures are now a genuine political force" (Paris and Ault 2004: 404). Defined by their antagonism to neoliberalism (rather than their style or music), they can become "new protest formations," practicing radical democracy internally and sometimes coalescing into disruptive street demonstrations (Marchart 2004).

SUCCESS?

Hopefully you now have a sense of the breadth of subcultural resistance. But are subculturists "successful" in resisting cultural and political hegemony? While it is unlikely that youth cultures will form the vanguard of a massive, radical revolution, I am not so cynical to believe that they can't be transformative for individuals, scenes, communities and, at times, societies. It is important to neither overestimate nor underestimate their significance. In the article "Did Punk Matter?" Kevin Mattson (2001: 74) argues that punk and riot grrrl were successful "experiments in alternative production and distribution of cultural products" in defiance of a corporate entertainment culture and that punks impacted politics in significant ways, especially at the local level. Successful resistance may be difficult to define, let alone measure, but many subculturists are certainly more than nihilistic hooligans or "harmless buffoons" (Hebdige 1979: 2).

KEY INSIGHTS

- Not all subculturists engage in active, overt resistance. Still, many subculturists challenge "the mainstream" through their music, styles, rituals, or via politicized lifestyles, and some engage directly in the political process as part of their subcultural identity.

- Some subculturists' beliefs and behaviors actually *reinforce* dominant ideologies and relationships.
- Subcultural resistance is complex and many-layered. Resistance occurs at the individual and societal levels, is experienced personally and collectively, and can be overt and/or covert.
- Subculturists rarely, if ever, seek to overthrow a government or to overturn the fundamental structures of society. However, neither should subcultures be dismissed as trivial fashion shows with no political significance.

EXPLORING FURTHER

Punk Record Labels and the Struggle for Autonomy: The Emergence of DIY, by Alan O'Connor, 2008 (Lexington Books). An insightful look into the business practices of "independent" record labels in Spain, Canada, and the US. Demonstrates how punks navigate between their anti-capitalist ideals and the capitalist world in which they live.

Senseless Acts of Beauty: Cultures of Resistance, by George McKay, 1996 (Verso). Explores the politics and political activities of a variety of countercultures since the 1970s, showing how DIY resistance did not end with hippies and punks.

"The Multidimensionality of Resistance in Youth-Subcultural Studies," by J. Patrick Williams, 2009 (*The Resistance Studies Magazine* 1: 20–33). A nice summary of the thinking around subcultural resistance. Available online.

Subcultures and Political Resistance, edited by Jeffrey Paris and Michael Ault, 2004. This special issue of *Peace Review* collects a variety of essays on subcultural politics,

Revolutionary Arab Rap, http://revolutionaryarabrap.blogspot.com. Very interesting blog about Arab rap and its connections to politics and revolution.

Sounds Like a Revolution, directed by Summer Love and Jane Michener, 2010. Documentary exploring the connections between music, youth scenes, and activism. Features interviews with and live footage of a variety of musician activists in the folk, punk, hip hop, rock, and country genres.

Pussy Riot: A Punk Prayer, directed by Mike Lerner and Maxim Pozdorovkin, 2013. This documentary chronicles the rise of feminist guerilla theater band/collective Pussy Riot, from their anti-Putin protests through several members' arrest and incarceration.

Positive Force: More Than a Witness, directed by Robin Bell, 2012. http://morethanawitness.com. Documents the 25-year history of the Washington, DC, punk activist collective Positive Force, an all-volunteer organization that has staged protests and raised money to fight homelessness, sexism, homophobia, hunger, and other social problems.

Taqwacore: The Birth of Punk Islam, directed by Omar Majeed, 2009. www.taqwacore.com. Documentary following the exploits of Islamic punk rockers as they tour the US, singing out against the excesses of both global capitalism and conservative Islam.

Heavy Metal in Baghdad, directed by Suroosh Alvi and Eddy Moretti, 2007. www.heavymetalinbaghdad.com. Documents the struggles of Iraqi metal band Acrassicauda as they pursue their musical passions in the midst of war.

4

WHO PARTICIPATES IN SUBCULTURES?

The iconic subculturist exemplifies the "spectacular" style subcultures studied by the Birmingham scholars, a lad who loves his music, his drink, and his mates. The skinhead with his cropped hair, braces, and steel-toed boots; the mod with his customized Vespa, a dozen shiny mirrors splaying out in a chrome fan from his motorbike; the punk sporting his leather jacket, safety-pin piercings, and "liberty spikes" haircut; the denim-clad, long-haired metalhead, his favorite band emblazoned across a black t-shirt. He is young, straight, white, and male, a marginalized "working-class hero" joined with his compatriots in defiance of an alienating, exploitative society. However, while certainly photogenic and not at all uncommon, this culture warrior hardly represents the variety of people identifying with subcultures in the twenty-first century. What types of people participate in subcultures? In previous chapters, I debunked the view of subculturists as psychologically disturbed or criminal youth and questioned the notion they are strictly the product of chaotic communities or "broken" homes. Subcultural participation is not confined to any particular psychological profile or demographic category; rather a diversity of people claim subcultural affiliations. Still, various groups may have different interest in, access to, and experiences within subcultural communities.

In this chapter, I explore how subcultural identities mesh and/or contend with other significant social identities such as race, social class, gender, and sexuality. Social scientists pay significant attention to race, class, and gender because these characteristics fundamentally influence our experiences and opportunities as human beings. For example, in many countries, one's race or ethnicity has profound consequences on one's educational opportunities, health, and even life expectancy. Because these identities play a central role in our lives they become contested terrain – subculturists, seeking alternatives to the "mainstream," often challenge these social building blocks. After all, what could be more subversive than gender bending, upending sexual norms, or challenging the class structure?

SOCIAL CLASS: ARE SUBCULTURISTS MOSTLY DISAFFECTED, WORKING-CLASS YOUTH?

In previous chapters, I showed how many scholars made strong connections between social class and subcultures; specifically, they argued that subcultures served as symbolic expressions of dissent by marginalized, mostly working-class youth. However, I would not be at all surprised if you know middle-class people who identify strongly with one subculture or another. Middle-class youth were involved in many of the seminal postwar subcultures, from hippies and punks to metal and hip hop, even if in some cases their more working-class peers outnumbered them. And the greater a subculture's longevity the more likely people from all walks of life will discover and join its ranks. In fact, subcultural participation may also offer the middle class relatively "safe" forms of rebellion, an opportunity to feel "different" without engaging in criminal or other activity that will jeopardize one's future (see Wilkins 2005).

Tattoo subcultures in many ways transcend social class, tattoos (at least good ones) having achieved the status of "art" (Kosut 2006). While tattoos have long served as marks of honor and status among cultures such as Māori, Samoa, and other Polynesian peoples, only recently have Western societies found tattoos acceptable on a grand scale. Previously viewed as low-class, tattoos have since become quite chic. That UK Prime Minister David Cameron's wife, Samantha, has a small dolphin tattooed on her foot hardly raises an eyebrow. (Although were she adorned with full tattoo sleeves, matters might be different!) The rise of suburban mall specialty stores such as Hot Topic that cater directly to subcultural sensibilities encourages and enables people from a range of classes to experiment with at least the stylistic elements of various subcultures.

By pointing out that subculturists belong to all social classes I am not suggesting that social class has no bearing on subcultural participation (see Shildrick and MacDonald 2006). Middle- and upper-class kids have, on average, greater opportunities to participate in conventional activities (travel, extracurricular activities) and adopt conventional identities (athlete, fashionista), as well as greater access to a good education and meaningful work. Therefore they may have stronger connections with and reasons to support the status quo. And certainly social class influences *how* people participate. While many affluent professionals are Harley-Davidson enthusiasts, the so-called one-percenters of true criminal motorcycle gangs likely draw support from among the less educated and less well-off. Money opens doors to certain kinds of subcultural participation, from travelling to Japan, Samoa, Thailand, and Hawaii to be tattooed to collecting rare, original-pressing records. Likewise, lack of funds curtails certain aspects of subcultural participation.

Being from a lower social class can also mark some subculturists for persecution (see Chapter 6), as social class has strong cultural meanings. Middle-class youth in Britain use the derogatory "chav" to distinguish themselves from their working-class peers, marking themselves as smarter, more morally upstanding, and more stylish and sophisticated (Hollingworth and Williams 2009). The white working class (especially in the absence of large racial minorities) becomes the "Other":

> What makes the 'chav' or 'charver' discourse so powerful, under the guise of either harmless light entertainment or unreflective, uncritical social science, is its role in pinning the mass of young, poor, white, working-class people to the social pathologies of ... welfare dependency, moral degeneracy, academic failure, fecklessness, and excessive and tasteless consumption.
>
> (Shildrick et al. 2009: 460–461)

The US equivalents might include "trailer trash," "white trash," or "welfare queen." The effect is to shore up class boundaries, especially given the economic uncertainty felt by many middle-class families. Even liberal, seemingly open-minded middle-class people talk about the chavs with a certain disdain, while conservatives openly view them with contempt as the word becomes a code for the undeserving poor (Jones 2012). No wonder then that some working-class youth might join together to defend and valorize their identities, much like the Chicago or Birmingham School scholars suggest.

CHAVS AND THE MARKERS OF CLASS

Social class has *cultural* as well as *economic* meanings and boundaries, particularly around style, behavior, and perceived morality (Hollingworth and Williams 2009). Fashions and brands have no *inherent* class meanings. Yet middle-class people denigrate tracksuits, peak hats, fake designer clothing, and large, "tacky" jewelry as the realm of tasteless charvers (Jones 2012). Social class does not dictate behavior, but people interpret behavior as indicative of class, seeing chavs as loud, crass, cocky, violence-prone, and criminal. People of all classes might have moral shortcomings, but so-called chavs face stereotypes of being irresponsible, disruptive, and disinterested in school. As in the case of racial minorities, the more privileged frame working class marginalization as a result of cultural failings rather than structural inequalities, racism, or classism.

RACE: DO SUBCULTURES MODEL RACIAL HARMONY OR PERPETUATE RACIAL DISCORD?

Race, and racism, are core features of social life, present to some degree in all contemporary cultures. In most societies, race, ethnicity, and religion *fundamentally* organize human experience – and conflict, considering the violence between Hutus and Tutsis in Rwanda, Shia and Sunni in Iraq, and blacks and whites in the US. So how does race inform subcultural experience? Clearly people of all races participate in many subcultures. But do subculturists of different races participate together, or are scenes racially segregated? Having established the importance of resistance in the previous chapter, do subcultures resist or reinforce racial meanings and stereotypes?

Race includes the socially constructed meanings attributed to bodies, language, and other cultural norms. Many societies create racial categories primarily according to skin color, and many people believe different races have *inherently* different aptitudes, interests, and morals; dominant groups often stereotype racial minorities as lazy, criminal, welfare dependent and so on. However, there is no biological basis for racial classification. Jewish people and the Romani peoples of Europe may have light skin tones yet remain targets of racism. In the early twentieth century, US law did not consider Italians, Irish, and other light skinned groups "white." In racially diverse Brazil, "black" and "white" have much more complex meanings than in the US, as education and wealth can "change" one's race (Braxton n.d.). In large part, powerful groups have created race to expand and preserve their own dominance. Despite the illusion of race, racist attitudes and, more importantly, histories of racist discrimination have in many nations resulted in **racial segregation**, or the systematic separation of peoples based upon racial categories. Segregation can be institutionalized by law, as in the former apartheid regime in South Africa or Jim Crow laws in the US, but in contemporary liberal democracies more often results from historical legacies of discrimination. Even children, who initially have no conception of race, often self-segregate into racially homogenous groups as they age.

In such contexts, subcultures might appear to be "racial enclaves." Particularly in majority group dominated areas, communities of color may seem subcultural simply by virtue of their minority status, for example Korean youth in Tokyo or the Chinese community in San Francisco. (However, such groups are not automatically subcultural in the sense I use the term.) Lowrider culture in the southwest US – built around classic cars with custom wheels, paint jobs, and often loud stereos and hydraulic suspensions – has long been associated with Chicano culture more generally. Lowriders (as participants are called) use cruising spaces and parking lots as leisure sites, discussing not only cars but also issues of broader significance to the Chicano community, creating spaces of both resistance and belonging (Chappell 2012).

The "racial enclave" vision of subcultures seems even more valid when participation hinges upon membership in a perceived racial category; a variety of subcultures espouse overtly racist ideologies, including White Power skinhead, nationalist black metal, and some football hooligans/ultras. More benignly, perhaps certain subcultures emerge as expressions of **homology**, or "the symbolic fit between the values and lifestyles of a group, its subjective experience and the musical forms it uses to express or reinforce its focal concerns" (Hebdige 1979: 143). So if hip hop and blues are inextricably bound to African American history and experience, then others cannot truly participate. Blacks can better understand and perform hip hop and only Japanese people can create and appreciate authentic anime. However, such a theory risks essentializing race, reinforcing narrow meanings of authenticity, and homogenizing the experiences of people in racial categories.

MULTICULTURAL SUBCULTURES: HOW DO SUBCULTURES CHALLENGE RACIAL IDEOLOGIES?

On the other hand, subcultures seem to blur racial boundaries, as in progressive rave, graffiti, b-boy, and queer scenes. Subcultures can offer spaces to disrupt racial norms. Scholars in the CCCS tradition noted that white working class youth adopted elements of "black" culture from West Indian immigrants (e.g. Hebdige 1979). Some subcultures offered up images of racial harmony: the Two-Tone era of ska featured multiracial bands and audiences, the Northern Soul scene esteemed black soul musicians, and even the notoriously white American hardcore scene drew major inspiration from the black Rastafari group Bad Brains. Thus people of color were instrumental in many post-WWII subcultures, although their contributions have often been minimized or ignored. Perhaps youth culture holds the key to racial harmony as young people share music, style, and other interests regardless of racial or class background. Hip hop may appear to be the quintessential case. What began as an urban movement among black and Latino youth made its way to Native American reservations on the plains of South Dakota with groups such as Native Era and The Grind Klick. Even as mainstream rap regularly offers up racial stereotypes for whites' consumption, underground hip hop scenes can provide multicultural spaces built around love of music and aesthetic but also the unity ideal. Yet truly multicultural subcultural spaces are rare; even the progressive and diverse underground hip hop scene in San Francisco is not truly colorblind, as "people with different racial identities ... engage hip hop in remarkably divergent ways" (Harrison 2009: 12).

While many white subculturists espouse a "colorblind" inclusivity, in reality, racial majority groups dominate many scenes, both numerically and in terms of influence. In response, people of color often carve out their own place within white-dominated scenes. Chicago hardcore punk band Los Crudos performed songs such as "We're That Spic Band" and "500 Años," singing primarily in Spanish about imperialism and inequality. Latino punks and hardcore kids have organized many Latino punk festivals in places such as Los Angeles and Chicago. Subcultures can also be sites of overt resistance to racism and discrimination, as when conscious hip hop artists such as dead prez and Immortal Technique critique racial profiling, racist discrimination, and the prison system, or when French and North African emcees challenge anti–immigrant sentiments. Chinese-American rapper MC Jin exalts his Chinese heritage while throwing racist stereotypes back at his listeners in the track "Learn Chinese."

WHO GETS TO USE THE N-WORD?

Cultural commentators, black intellectuals, and hip hop artists alike periodically wring their hands over the question of who, if anyone, can legitimately use the word "nigger" or, more commonly, "nigga." Opponents view the word as degrading and racist regardless of speaker or context, while proponents reclaim "nigga" to disrupt its original racist connotations. The debate rages even among black intellectuals, often along class lines, pitting what sociologist Michael Eric Dyson (2006) calls the "Afristocracy" against the "Ghettocracy." But what do hip hop subculturists think in the context of their local scenes? Geoff Harkness (2008) finds that blacks in Chicago's hip hop scene are "allowed" to use the word with impunity, for whites it remains taboo, and Latinos can use the word under certain circumstances. These rules help maintain boundaries of authenticity as people of all racial backgrounds appropriate hip hop; black equals real, white equals fake, the ability to use the n-word reinforces who is real and fake. Latino rappers can use the word because many share blacks' history of struggle, marginalization, and resistance and because Latinos (especially Puerto Ricans) were instrumental in hip hop's origins. For a few participants even disadvantaged whites who are "hood" share important experiences with blacks and may, therefore, deploy the n-word. A Latino person can be "black," a disadvantaged white can be a "white nigga." Interestingly, in disconnecting racial labels from essentialist, biological qualities such as skin color these hip hoppers inadvertently reveal the *social construction* of race.

WHITENESS

Just as subcultures serve as spaces for racial and ethnic minorities to interrogate racist stereotypes and inequalities, so too are they spaces to perform "whiteness." Avowedly racist subculturists such as Nazi skinheads denigrate racial minorities, labeling them as biologically, culturally, and morally inferior. But in so doing they also paint a certain (righteous) portrait of whites as superior. "Hatecore" metal – the North American counterpart to National Socialist black metal in Europe – very strategically uses music to market its brand of pan-Aryanism, cleverly cloaking white racialist and anti-Semitic themes in more palatable motifs of paganism, national myths, and defense against unnamed "enemies" common in other forms of metal (Hochhauser 2011).

Racist ideologies congeal around the **white racial frame**, "an overarching worldview, one that encompasses important racial ideas, terms, images, emotions, and interpretations" and is the lens through which most whites and those conforming to white norms see race (Feagin 2010: 3). The white racial frame explains why many whites in the US believe, regardless of empirical data that paint a more nuanced picture, that immigrants drain public resources, escalate crime rates, and "steal" "their" jobs. Whiteness is rarely questioned, rarely problematized, but is rather taken for granted, the "norm" to which racial minorities are compared. White is good, clean, pure, while black is evil, dirty, corrupted. Whiteness offers unearned entitlement, or white privilege. The white racial frame is pervasive; racism is not simply a "sickness" to be excised from an otherwise healthy social body. Rather, racism is embedded in and fundamental to the social order (Feagin 2010).

The consumption and performance of narrow (often stereo-typical) slices of "black" culture reinforces perceptions of whiteness as safe, rule-abiding, and normal. As perhaps the most stigmatized group in the US, black men represent danger and freedom, but also cool and sexually potency (West 2001). White parents may react with alarm as their children adopt modes of speech and dress perceived as belonging to youth of color. For some white kids then, shedding their "whiteness" becomes part of their performance of "cool." In fact, part of white youths' rebellion has often included appropriating artistic and subcultural practices from communities of color (Kitwana 2005). Subcultures may provide white kids with opportunities to safely "play" with whiteness and consume cultural phenomena connected with people of color, while leaving racist ideologies largely unquestioned. Such sharing (or appropriating) can inadvertently reinforce the white racial frame, "proving" that racial egalitarianism, rather than racial inequality, is the norm, that everyone "gets along" just fine. Predominately white, middle-class subcultures such as goth may offer whites a chance to demonstrate their progressive, multicultural attitudes without really sacrificing any of their privilege (see Wilkins 2008).

Many seemingly pluralist societies view open, blatant racism with disdain and intimations of white racial superiority as backward. Where racist slurs are shameful, racism has transformed into a more subtle form of racism based not upon theories of genetic superiority, but instead on *moral* or *cultural* difference. Such **colorblind racism**, or "racism without racists," tends to hold that racial prejudice and discrimination are largely over; that the worst of racism (e.g. slavery) was in the past and has little bearing on the present; and that any remaining racial inequality is the fault of minority groups who simply have not worked hard enough (Bonilla-Silva 2009). Shades of colorblind racism frequently emerge in predominately white "hipster" scenes in the form of "ironic" race-based jokes about "thugs" or acoustic covers of gangsta rap songs, meant to communicate one's progressive racial consciousness but actually reinforcing both whiteness and otherness (West 2012). Hipster racism includes "ideas, speech, and action meant to deni-grate [another person's] race or ethnicity under the guise of being urbane, witty (meaning 'ironic' nowadays), educated, liberal, and/ or trendy" (Peterson 2008). Visiting a "shady" bar in a "ghetto" part of town as part of a nocturnal adventure qualifies, as does dressing as a "pimp" or "hoe" for Halloween. "Ironic racism," brushed off as "un-PC" (politically correct) but still harmless, often reinforces the very stereotypes it means to mock.

Despite the pervasiveness and persistence of the white racial frame, subcultures do, on occasion, join with others to offer a **counter-frame**, an alternative view protesting racist practices and exposing government repression. Chicago hardcore band Racetraitor vehemently confronted their predominately white audiences with critiques of colonialism, white privilege, and racist oppression, insightfully framing racism as a set of power relationships rather than simply personal attitudes (Peterson 2009). Seattle straight edge band Trial used their live shows to educate kids about the FBI's violent suppression of groups such as the Black Panther Party for Self Defense, while advocating for indigenous rights and freedom for political prisoners including the American Indian Movement's Leonard Peltier. Anti-racist skinheads and punks join Anti-Racist Action groups, passing out anti-racist literature at shows and Brazilian thrash metal legends Sepultura wrote songs about and advocated for indigenous rights.

GENDER: WHERE ARE ALL THE GIRLS?

In 1976, Vi Subversa, a middle-aged mother of two, cofounded anarchopunk band Poison Girls in Brighton, just prior to the Sex Pistols making punk a household word (Reddington 2007). The band espoused radical ideas, challenging government repression, sexual norms, and patriarchy, as in the song "Real Woman": "I'm not a real woman, I don't nod my head, and patiently wait, for your favors in bed. ... I'm not a real woman, I don't waggle my hips, or flap my eye lids, or shackle my lips." While many punk bands of the time included women, punk histories typically give men – the Sex Pistols, the Ramones, the Clash – all the credit for starting what became one of the most influential music revolutions of the past 100 years. At first glance, men seem to dominate many subcultures, both numerically and in terms of their influence. Skinhead, punk, hardcore, parkour, car cultures, metal, and so on all seem to attract more men than women. Goth, hip hop, indie, emo, and slam poetry may include relatively more women, but men still have disproportionate creative power, even in supposedly anti-sexist scenes. Why are there so few women in subcultures? Do subcultures offer women and men space to stretch the boundaries of masculinity and femininity?

The first explanation for the mystery of the "missing" subcultural women suggests that subcultures mirror the dominant social patterns of societies in general, at least in regard to gender, i.e. subcultures are patriarchal. Reminiscent of Chicago School and CCCS theories, British sociologist Mike Brake (1985) saw many subcultures as fundamentally masculinist because they were spaces where young, mostly working-class men found the status unavailable to them elsewhere. Subcultures *glorify* manliness. Women who *do* participate, participate as second-class citizens: male bikers in outlaw motorcycle gangs valued "biker mamas" and "old ladies" primarily for their sexual availability and ability to make money as strippers, making them "property" of the club (Hopper and Moore 1990). Further reflecting patriarchal cultures, perhaps girls have less disposable income to spend on concerts, records, motorbikes, and other subcultural paraphernalia, and parents might allow their daughters less freedom to go out at night, to hang out in clubs or on the streets. Instead of participating in spectacular youth cultures, girls form **bedroom cultures** in which they share pop culture fandom, fantasizing about actors and singers in the safety of their homes (McRobbie and Garber 1976). Girls swooning over actor Robert Pattinson (*Twilight*) or Columbian pop star Juanes hardly seem like a subculture, but such private spaces offer some space to explore sexuality without overt male judgment (Kearney 2006). While each of these explanations makes some sense, contemporary girls and women face fewer constraints than their counterparts of generations past, taking a much more active role in many scenes.

However, too often researchers have simply paid less attention to women in subcultures or have cast women only as accessories to men, dismissing their unique experiences (McRobbie 2000). Unfortunately women's contributions to subcultural history, like history in general, go largely unacknowledged. For example, while Sugarhill Gang recorded the first commercially successful rap song ("Rapper's Delight") and Grandmaster Flash and the Furious Five recorded the first conscious rap song ("The Message"), few know that each song owes a huge debt to producer, promoter, and label owner Sylvia Robinson (Watkins 2005). Her artistic instincts and connections in the radio and music worlds helped launch emceeing onto the international stage, eventually making rap music and hip hop culture into one of the most pervasive and influential scenes the world has known. Likewise with punk, fashion designer Vivienne Westwood's designs profoundly influenced the early punk aesthetic, and many early punk bands – the Raincoats, the Slits, and Poison Girls in the UK, Blondie, X-Ray Specs, X, Sonic Youth in the US – featured women (see Reddington 2007). Thus it is not that women were/are absent from subcultures, but rather that researchers have ignored or downplayed their participation.

In the face of patriarchal gender norms, sexist subcultural gate-keepers (e.g. record executives, promoters, music journalists, dee-jays), and even the disdain of their peers, women have asserted themselves within male-dominated scenes and have carved out "their own" subcultural spaces. The heavily masculinist metal scene has nevertheless produced Gallhammer, a Japanese all-woman metal/crust band; Canada's Mares of Thrace; and Sweden's Crucified Barbara. Riot grrrls started a revolution in punk, while science fiction, steampunk, and anime cosplay cultures have significant numbers of women. However, much like women athletes, women subculturists must often balance challenges to and performances of traditional femininities, combining tattoo sleeves with lipstick and sexual allure. Women, much more so than men, must prove they participate for the "right" reasons.

Women do constitute a majority in some subcultures. Burlesque, or neo-burlesque, involves women performing partial striptease routines, reveling in an ironic disruption of beauty standards and expectations of "appropriate" female sexuality (Nally 2009). Roller derby, a campy amateur sport in which roller-skating women crash into one another as they race around a track, pits teams against one another in "bouts" that often leave skaters bruised. Derby leagues proliferate from Australia to Dubai, include teams with colorful names such as Cupcake Cannibals and Dominate Tricks, and player pseudonyms like Countess of Crush and Anne Arkie. Japan's Lolita cultures involve mostly girls handcrafting elaborate, lacy Victorian-inspired costumes that transform the wearer into a living doll: "A Lolita's dress modestly conceals her mature body beneath ornately elaborate garments adorned with lace, ribbons, ruffles, and bows; she poses and conducts herself in order to create a surreal and fantastic childlike appearance" (Winge 2008: 50). Fan fiction, a mostly online subculture of writers sharing unauthorized stories based upon pop culture icons such as *Twilight*, *Harry Potter*, *Sailor Moon*, and even *Law & Order*, offers women a space to experiment with sexuality (Bury 2005). Many ficcers write sexually explicit "slash" stories, "ficships" depicting sexual relationships between characters such as Bella and Edward from the *Twilight* book and film series. Burlesque, roller derby, and fan fiction have long histories, but contemporary participants revive the past in third-wave feminist form.

WOMEN EMCEES IN JAPAN

Even though Japanese record executives regard young women as a key marketing demographic, the drivers of pop music consumption, they award few women recording contracts. Women emcees must navigate between the "cute," girlish aesthetic that dominates pop music, anime, and manga and the hypermasculine, hardcore images predominant in hip hop (Condry 2006). Nevertheless, some women rappers such as Ai and Miss Monday break away from the "cutismo" culture and sing songs about women's assertiveness and empowerment.

GENDER RESISTANCE OR REINFORCEMENT?

Gender and sexual norms – the "rules" of femininity and masculinity – are among the primary organizing principles of most cultures, making them ripe targets for subcultural resistance. Even as women of many nations gain greater political rights, they face significant backlash from conservative forces that see changing roles as a threat to the "natural" order (i.e. patriarchy). Part of what made hippies such a "threat" (aside from their drug use) was women's newfound (if limited) sexual liberation and men's eschewing of the patriarchal breadwinner role. As I noted in the previous chapter, subcultures tend to simultaneously resist and reinforce cultural standards. In dressing modestly, if flamboyantly, do Japan's Lolitas resist the sexualization of women? Does their style "become objects of visual resistance against acceptable norms of dress and all that these norms stand for" (Winge 2008: 59)? Lolitas, despite many

Lolis' intentions, become sexual fetishes for adult Japanese men. Yet Theresa Winge (2008: 60) argues that the aesthetic "creates a safe space to be sexy and strong behind the protection of the childhood patina." Similarly, kogals – seemingly shallow, materialistic, and self-centered – may offer young Japanese women a degree of cultural power, presenting a "symbolic inversion" that "inverts cultural models or presents an alternative to them" (Miller 2004: 242). They challenge the "restraint, docility, modesty, and elegance" expected of Japanese women, expectations that reinforce male privilege and patriarchy (Miller 2004: 242).

Burlesque performers enact "patterns of resistance against an oppressive concept of 'pure,' 'true,' and 'respectable' femininity" (Willson 2008: 6), challenging "the general idea of the suppression of female sexuality, the expectation that women are chaste and have no sexual desires outside of heteronormative relations" (Nally 2009: 623). As a full-contact sport, roller derby erases any lingering notions that women are delicate or frail, as well as satirizing bodies and sexualities via sexual innuendo. Rather than passively absorbing pop culture, fan fic writers transform the object of their fandom, sometimes in subversive ways; *Twilight*, often criticized by feminists for romanticizing abuse and glorifying virginity, can become a racy, hypersexual, queering playground in the hands of a ficcer. Women gamers face significant discrimination in the video game world; their mere presence in such a male-dominated space defies the rules and expectations for women and men (Kennedy 2005). They resist by forming female-only teams, creating women-run gaming servers, refusing to be pushed out by men, and simply by being successful in aggressive, violent games (Delamere and Shaw 2008).

In the early 1990s, riot grrrl became one of the most influential subcultures as bands such as Bikini Kill and Bratmobile and 'zines such as *Riot Grrrl* and *Jigsaw* sought a feminist "Revolution Girl Style Now" within the punk/indie scene. Challenging sexism and patriarchy both within punk and without, riot grrrls brought a DIY ethic to media production as they drew attention to sexual assault, domestic violence, eating disorders, reproductive rights, and body shame (Piano 2003; Kaltefleiter 2009). 'Zine making became an act of resistance (Schilt 2003). Riot grrrls founded women's music festivals and facilitated workshops and other gatherings, sort of punk rock versions of the feminist consciousness raising groups of the 60s. As they played shows with "slut" or "bitch" written on their bodies, riot grrrls forcefully contested the virgin/whore dichotomy forced upon women (Attwood 2007; Leonard 1997). Even as the culture industry coopted "girl power" into the Spice Girls and Pussycat Dolls, riot grrrl lives on in feminist politics such as "slutwalk" protest movements whereby women challenge the victim-blaming surrounding sexual assault and march for legislative change.

Subcultures do often provide women tools to challenge, resist, and playfully satirize patriarchal expectations of women. While far from feminist utopias, such subcultures offer women tools of cultural resistance and networks of support in societies that too often pit women against one another.

NEW MASCULINITIES?

Subcultures also provide spaces for men to both contest and reinforce dominant masculine norms. While many subcultures have been hypermasculine hangouts dominated by men, some encourage men to challenge **hegemonic masculinity**, the most valued, highest status cultural ideals of male identity and behavior by which all men are measured. Expected to be strong, independent, aggressive, good looking, straight, sexually powerful, in control, hardworking, and successful, men live under a constant "burden of proof" (Kimmel 1996). "Emo" boys have become something of a cliché, often mocked by other subculturists for their emotional displays, songs of love, loneliness, and loss, occasional eyeliner and nail polish, dramatic fashions, and other perceived feminine qualities (see Bailey 2005). Yet emo may be a contemporary response to an ongoing **crisis of masculinity** in which men struggle with the meanings of manhood as the structural foundations of patriarchal masculinity – breadwinning, occupational success, women's subordination, and straight sexuality – erode (see Williams 2007). "Nerdcore," a rap subgenre characterized by lyrics about video games, comic books, *Star Wars*, and all things nerdy, flies in the face of hypermasculine gangsta rap, seemingly undermining "hard" masculinity (Ronald 2012).

Similarly to women's subcultural resistance, men's gender resistance produces mixed results. In abstaining from alcohol, tobacco, eating meat, and sexual conquest, straight edge men seemingly resist several hallmarks of young masculinity (Haenfler 2004a). However, the scene also fosters a hypermasculine side based upon glorifying "hardness" and "control" (Purchla 2011). Straight edge men compare themselves favorably to the "going rate" of masculinity, extolling "unity" and claiming the scene is more egalitarian than mainstream culture, other scenes, and than the hardcore scene was in the past (Mullaney 2007). Yet women face their own "burden of proof" as men question their motivations and commitment and often exclude them from full participation. Likewise, nerdcore challenges hegemonic masculinities, but if audiences perceive white emcees' performances as simple parody of black performers, the genre risks reinforcing the white racial frame. And finally, male skaters may resist the competition, domination, and "jock" attitudes inherent in so many sports while still seeing skateboarding as a primarily male activity (Beal 1996).

SEXUALITY

In the past 60 years, effective birth control, women's economic empowerment, and feminist and queer movements have fuelled a sexual revolution that in the span of only a few generations has significantly changed how people *think* about sex, how/why/with whom they *have* sex, and how people express their sexual *identities*. Subculturists have often been among the first to openly proclaim the virtues of sex for pure pleasure rather than procreation or marital obligation. The Beats of the 1950s along with the 1960s counterculture professed a new sexual liberation captured in the slogan "free love." However, such liberation mostly afforded *straight men* greater sexual freedoms, reinforcing a sexual double standard marking prolific men as "studs" and sexually active women as "sluts." Derby girls, burlesquers, ficcers, and riot grrrls' performances of sexuality call into question the virgin/whore dichotomy.

SUICIDEGIRLS.COM – "EMPOWERED EROTICA" OR ALT-PORN?

Tired of the narrow portrayal of feminine beauty found in mainstream media, Suicide Girls founder Missy Suicide began the site as a DIY experiment in women's empowerment. Suicide Girls features nude pin ups of tattooed and pierced goth/punk/indie/metal women, often with dyed hair cut in edgy styles. Seeking to "redefine beauty," Suicide Girls lets girls express themselves via blogs and profiles. They earn a small amount of money, more if they go on tour. The site has spawned a lucrative industry including live burlesque tours, comic books, apparel, and news, celebrity interviews, and gaming articles. So is Suicide Girls "empowered erotica" or "alt porn"? Meant to embody unbridled creativity, individuality, and sexual expressiveness, famous SGs such as Australian musician Brody Dalle symbolize, as one SG puts it, "finding your own ideals within yourself and becoming that, instead of relying on conditioning" (Diehl 2007: 210). Yet is the site really so different from the *Girls Gone Wild* series featuring inebriated college-aged "mainstream" women baring their bodies for men's consumption? Suicide Girls captures the tension between subcultural resistance and reinforcement of dominant standards of gender and sexuality. No doubt many participants *do* feel empowered, even resistant of the "body hatred" so prevalent amongst young women (see Frost 2001). However, most participants conform to the slender, fine-featured, young, and *white* standards of beauty found in mainstream fashion magazines (Magnet 2007). Their bodies, and their beauty, constitute "body projects" requiring attention to and tinkering with the body to a much greater degree than that required of young men. Their demure yet seductive poses come straight from more conventional pornography and they remain commercial objects of sexual desire while earning little money themselves (Healey 2005). Models have complained of mistreatment and the organization has faced criticism for falsely passing itself off as woman-owned. Suicide Girls exemplifies a larger pattern of young women using sexuality to get the attention of young men (Levy 2006), not because they are insecure, opportunistic, or otherwise individually flawed, but because they live in societies that too often teach women to gauge their worth according to the sexual approval of men.

Despite their image of sexual permissiveness, many subcultures are **heterocentrist** – upholding the "normalcy" of heterosexuality – at best, and actively **homophobic** – actively marginalizing of gay people – at worst. Heavy metal and hip hop, two of the most widespread subcultures in the world, have exceptionally homophobic and heterocentrist themes. Pop music in general celebrates straight sexuality. Despite increasing visibility and acceptance of queer identities in some parts of the world, the dominant **sexual script** of one man, one woman, both attractive and of similar ages, in an ongoing relationship, continues to be the standard by which all sexual expression is judged.

Like women, lesbians, gays, bisexuals, transgenders, and queers (LGBTQs) have often had to fight for recognition in existing subcultures. Hardcore scenes have spawned "queercore" or "homocore" contingents, including straight edge band Limp Wrist, whose song "I Love Hardcore Boys" directly challenges hardcore's straight hypermasculinity (see Kuhn 2010). Queercore "queers" punk but also "punks" queer, as anti-corporate and DIY culture serves as a "tactically playful" vehicle for queer politics (DeChaine 1997). Via records, live performances, and "queerzines," queercore challenged not only the hegemonic sexual script but also "mainstream" gay and lesbian groups dominated by middle-class whites seeking assimilation (Du Plessis and Chapman 1997). Queer sensibilities of camp and drag infuse goth, riot grrrl, and club scenes, while drag queens and kings form subcultures into themselves (Taylor 2012b). Such efforts have also produced queer contingents in steampunk and, more recently, hip hop, as artists such as Le1f garner international attention and hip hop heavyweights such as Jay-Z argue for greater inclusivity (Van Meter 2012). There have even been factions of queer skinheads!

Queer is more than a take-back word meant to transform a hurtful epithet into a defiant identity. Although queer has become an umbrella term for all non-normative sexual identities and practices, its roots are more radical. Queer movements and subcultures abhor rigid, binary categories such as male/female, gay/straight, celebrating rebellion and instability rather than seeking assimilation of LGBTQ people into heteronormative structures such as marriage. Instead of broadening the notion of "normal," queer questions the very notion of normality, clearly connecting with many subcultural politics. To "queer" something is to investigate the taken-for-granted, to interrogate power, especially regarding the "proper" use of bodies and identities. Queer subcultures, especially lesbian and transgender cultures, call into question theories and histories focused almost exclusively on young, white, working class, straight men (Halberstam 2005). Drag kings, for example, present "female masculinities," separating masculinity from male bodies (Halberstam 1998). Because gender and sexual ideologies are so intertwined, queer subculturists challenge both. Gay male cultures often fetishize hard, muscular bodies as well as masculinist norms such as sexual confidence and assertiveness. With their heavy eyeliner, long bangs, and slender bodies, gay youth who identify with emo aesthetics perform a more androgynous masculinity (Peters 2010).

Prior to the gay liberation movements of the 1950s and 1960s, urban gay communities may have constituted subcultures in and of themselves, drawn together by consistent persecution and the need for safe, affirming space. As I've shown above, queer sensibilities and identities have been incorporated into both pop and subcultural spaces. I would argue that, much like communities of color, gays and lesbians as a whole no longer constitute a subculture, even as they often display subcultural traits. However, certain subcultures are inextricably queer. In the vogueing ball culture of New York, primarily black and Latino gay and trans men "walk" a runway (catwalk) in drag, competing for prizes in categories from "vogue femme" to "butch queen in pumps." Drag kings and queens have a long subcultural history (Rupp and Taylor 2003), and some burlesque performers cross dress, queering gender and sexual identities (Nally 2009). The larger gay scene fosters a variety of subcultures (see Taylor 2012b). Subcultures within the larger gay community abound – "bears," full-figured gay men known for their facial hair and hairy bodies, have cultivated their own events, vernacular, and aesthetic, often portraying a more conventionally masculine image.

Queer cultures have in turn influenced other subcultures. Anarchists often combine anarchism with queer politics, finding synchronicity between anarchism's commitment to autonomy and abhorrence of hierarchy and queer questioning of sexual power. Some refuse marriage as a patriarchal, capitalist institution, others explore polyamory and bisexuality, seeing their practices as disrupting "the discourse of normative sexuality, and the relations of power it supports" (Portwood-Stacer 2010: 485).

KEY INSIGHTS

- Subcultural participation extends across all demographic categories. There is no singular profile of a "typical" subculturist.
- Race, class, gender, and sexual identity profoundly impact our life chances and give shape to dominant ideologies and power relations, making such characteristics important sites of subcultural resistance.
- Subculturists tend to both contest *and* reinforce established social hierarchies. To suggest that subcultural resistance on these fronts is revolutionary may be naïve, but to call such resistance meaningless is overly cynical and denies subculturists' subjective experience.
- Women and queer-identified subculturists both demand spaces within existing subcultures as well as creating more welcoming subcultures adjacent to established scenes.
- Subcultures can serve as multicultural experiments or racist enclaves, and can support or subvert a white racial frame. Many tend to align along racial categories.

EXPLORING FURTHER

Next Wave Cultures: Feminism, Subcultures, Activism, edited by Anita Harris, 2008 (Routledge). A collection of essays exploring how contemporary young women enter masculine domains, carve out their own subcultural spaces, and engage in activism.

The Lost Women of Rock Music: Female Musicians of the Punk Era, by Helen Reddington, 2007 (Ashgate). A cultural history of women in early UK punk rock and their exclusion from many punk histories, including interviews from musicians and other insiders.

Lowrider Space: Aesthetics and Politics of Mexican American Custom Cars, by Ben Chappell, 2012 (University of Texas Press). An ethnography of a Mexican American lowrider scene in Austin, Texas.

Hip Hop Underground: The Integrity and Ethics of Racial Identification, by Anthony Kwame Harrison, 2009 (Temple University Press). An ethnography of San Francisco Bay area hip hop that captures the complexity of race in hip hop and questions the "colorblindness" of the seemingly racially aware scene.

The Hip Hop Wars: What We Talk About When We Talk About Hip Hop – And Why it Matters, by Tricia Rose, 2008 (Basic-Civitas Books). Discusses the top ten debates in hip hop, including hip hop's relationship to violence and misogyny, while also offering progressive visions of what hip hop is and might be.

Playing It Queer: Popular Music, Identity, and Queer World-Making, by Jodie Taylor, 2012 (Peter Lang Publishers). A wide-ranging book connecting music and subcultures to queer politics and identities, from queercore and riot grrrl to drag kings and queens.

Hip Hop: Beyond Beats and Rhymes, directed by Byron Hurt, 2006. A documentary investigating misogyny, violence, homophobia, and masculinity in hip hop.

Paris is Burning, directed by Jennie Livingston, 1990. An award-winning documentary about the New York City drag ball culture, in which black, Latino, gay, and transgendered participants walk runways, pose, and "vogue" as they compete for trophies in various categories. Explores race, class, and gender issues while revealing an important queer subculture.

American Juggalo, directed by Sean Dunne, 2011. www.americanjuggalo.com. A short film that captures the familial and even neo-tribal aspects of fans of Insane Clown Posse, many of whom feel socially alienated.

Beyond The Screams: A US Latino Hardcore Punk Documentary, directed by Martin Sorrondeguy, 1999. DIY documentary chronicling the growth of Latino hardcore in the US but also showing punk's emergence in Latin America. Available on YouTube and Google video.

5

WHO ARE THE "AUTHENTIC" PARTICIPANTS AND WHO ARE THE "POSEURS"?

Sometime in the early 2000s I went to several hardcore and punk shows at a "venue" called the Junkyard. The site had earned its name by being an actual junkyard, strewn with stacks of decomposing auto carcasses and surrounded by a chain link fence. In the midst of the wreckage stood a small machine shop in which the owner of the yard, an old punk, stripped cars of their parts for customers in need of repairs. On the night of a show, he cleared the shop floor to make space for bands, merch tables, and a mosh pit. The Junkyard was in a polluted, industrial suburb of Denver, Colorado, past a row of mobile homes and in sight of an enormous oil refinery. Difficult to find, only those "in the know" were likely to ever attend. In short, the Junkyard was the perfect place to see underground, no-frills, "authentic" DIY punk and hardcore; no one was making much money, the bands and kids were there for the love of music and the hardcore community.

At one particular show a young man, perhaps 17 years old, stood out even amongst the motley group of punks and hardcore kids usually in attendance. He expertly dressed the part of a 77-style punk: tall, red mohawk/mohican hair, torn jeans, safety pins through his ears, and a black leather jacket with an anarchy "A" scrawled on its back. While he displayed all the accoutrements of a working-class squatter punk from an era long past, it was almost as if he were trying *too* hard to prove his "punkness." After the show, he and a few friends walked towards the parking area to find their car. I watched in disbelief as he unlocked a *brand new BMW* sedan, and he and his entourage drove home to a presumably much nicer part of town.

In this chapter, I reveal the many ways in which subculturists construct authenticity by cultivating "subcultural capital" such as specialized knowledge (e.g. subcultural history), possession of "sacred" objects (e.g. extensive record collection, rare Vespa scooter), style (e.g. tattoos, piercings, hair and clothing) and perceived commitment (e.g. longevity in the scene). I then consider the impact of commercialization and commodification on subcultural experience and authenticity, suggesting that as the market appropriates and sells underground ideas and practices scenes respond by returning to and reinvigorating original subcultural ideals.

AUTHENTICITY: HOW DO SUBCULTURISTS JUDGE WHAT IS "REAL" AND "TRUE"?

Subculturists might only rarely speak directly about authenticity, but many still divide people, practices, and objects into cool/true/real and lame/false/fake. **Authenticity** requires that we actually be the sort of person we want others to perceive us to be. Pursuing, performing, and judging authenticity is central to most subcultural experience (and to human experience generally). We use authenticity to express ideals – made cynical by politicians perceived as phony, some voters seek out "authentic" candidates, concerned, in some cases, more by their "realness" than their actual policy positions. We also use authenticity to communicate status. For example, people judge "good" and "bad" music in part on its perceived authenticity. Good music is original, creative, truthful, and performed by technically competent musicians. Bad music is mass-produced, artificial, formulaic, and commercially driven – think *Pop Idol* in the UK and its US and India counterparts *American Idol* and *Indian Idol* (see Frith 1978; Washburne and Derno 2004). But who decides what is "the real deal" and what is fake? Music and art critics, cultural commentators, and academics might all express opinions about a subculture's authenticity, but more important is how subculturists determine who is "true" and who is a "poseur."

The first insight to remember about authenticity is that there is no such thing as authenticity. You might bristle at the suggestion that your favorite *Idol* is somehow less authentic than the latest underground artists. Your definition of good music might differ from others, and you might even appreciate the *Idols* that come from humble backgrounds, working their way up from nothing to pop music stardom. The point being that people interpret the same person/situation/object – and judge its authenticity – quite differently. **Authenticity is a social construction**, given meaning only by the people to whom it is meaningful (see Vannini and Williams 2009). It includes shared (and contested) meanings created in relationships, not an objective set of criteria. Has an underground rap artist who chooses to sign to a major record label sold out? Some hip hop heads would say "yes," others might say "it depends," while others would claim "of course not," suggesting that authenticity has more to do with lyrical content than a record label; "different kinds of audiences approach the issue of authenticity with varying degrees of intensity and focus, and sometimes rely on contradictory sets of criteria when evaluating a particular place or performance" (Grazian 2003: 22). Still, despite the messiness of "evaluating" authenticity, most scenes have at least *some* consensus around meaningful criteria. But such criteria are neither permanent nor universally understood or accepted (Peterson 2005).

A second insight is that **authenticity is an ongoing process**, not an achievement. Subculturists engage in "authenticity work" while avoiding the appearance of caring about authenticity (Peterson 2005). In other words, subculturists always, in certain contexts, have something to prove, no matter their previous status or achievements. Authenticity is situational, dependent upon the people and their interactions in a certain time and place. For example, street artists such as Shepard Fairey and Banksy gained worldwide reputations as subversive graffiti writers who painted or pasted their artwork in public places without permission, often with the goal of disrupting the consciousness of passersby. Fairey famously created the "Andre the Giant has a Posse" sticker campaign, while Banksy surreptitiously placed his own art in New York's Museum of Modern Art, making both legends in the underground street art subculture. Yet their notoriety eventually translated into a degree of fame and financial success, bringing with it charges of selling out. Fairey's work hangs in the Smithsonian, the National Portrait Gallery (the Obama "Hope" portrait), and a variety of other prestigious (and mainstream) museums. Banksy's work regularly sells for hundreds of thousands of pounds. However, perhaps both artists gain back a certain level of street cred by continuing to spread anti-authoritarian messages, raising money for progressive causes, and, in the case of Banksy, remaining anonymous. Authenticity isn't a permanent, objective status one gains and then enjoys. At the risk of being repetitive, authenticity is contextual; its meaning and evaluation depend upon the people and the social contexts in which they make such judgments.

This relates to a third insight, that subculturists often self-consciously **perform authenticity**. It can take a lot of thought and effort to seem cool. Consider the ongoing "hipster" scene. (I won't call hipsters a subculture for reasons discussed in Chapter 1.) Beyond their vague appreciation for independent music, various alternative lifestyles, and appreciation of irony, contemporary hipsters are difficult to describe. On top of that, few, if any, people self-identify as hipsters and others scenesters commonly use the term pejoratively. (Of course judgments of so-called hipsters as shallow trend-followers reflect observers' biases and constructions of authenticity!) Yet a variety of tastes and practices have become associated with "hipster" scenes, wrapped into an obsession with authenticity. Just a few things that have taken on hipster cache: "dive" bars; beards and/or odd moustaches; vintage pop culture references (e.g. old cartoons, toys); obscure, independent films; cursive-script tattoos; and a general disdain for mass-marketed pop culture. The hipster performance, it seems, is ironic, self-deprecating, and retro/vintage, while also communicating being "in the know." I once heard a friend joke about how much effort hipsters put into looking unkempt. On the other hand, some subculturists demonstrate their authenticity by *avoiding* spectacular displays of style and taste, focusing instead on cultivating a philosophical commitment to creativity, compassion, and self-actualization (Lewin and Williams 2009). Tired of scene politics and fashions, many become critical of such performances (perhaps especially as they age), making authenticity an anti-performance (Haenfler 2012a).

Finally, authenticity constitutes part of a larger process of internal **hierarchy** and external **boundary making**. Internally, few subcultures have rigid hierarchies, but authenticity helps participants police appropriate or desirable behavior, to be sure people are present for the "right" reasons. Widdicombe and Wooffitt (1995: 157) write, "It is not what a person does that makes her a genuine person, but what informs or motivates her actions." In other words, dressing up like a goth, *doing* goth, isn't enough; *being* goth requires the right motivations. Externally, battles over the shifting criteria for authenticity help subculturists construct a collective identity, a sense of "us" and "them." Evaluations of authenticity help subcultures keep undesirable people out, and offer clues to outsiders who want to get in (how to behave, how to look, which beliefs to profess). This may seem counterintuitive given many subculturists' effort to form inclusive, less hierarchical communities. (Also, I don't mean to imply subcultures always have readily identifiable boundaries.) But status and boundaries are ubiquitous in human life, even though groups perpetuate different levels of status inequality and boundaries may be either rigid or diffuse. Boundaries may be necessary, or functional, to the extent they distinguish subculturists from outsiders, providing ways to say "This is who *we* are, and who we are is more 'real' than the commercial, conformist, boring, or oppressive world out there." If anyone and anything can be goth, then being goth means nothing. The ongoing conversation about what constitutes goth reminds current and potential adherents that the identity holds significant meaning, even if participants are wary of imposing too rigid or exclusive a definition, or if they grow weary of the "what is goth?" discussion. Subculturists complicate matters even more by often disliking labels. Not wanting to be classified, they profess their individuality, expressing "a true or inner self which just happens to reflect, or mesh with, the underlying values of the group" (Widdicombe and Wooffitt 1995: 157).

MAKING JUDGMENTS: WHAT ARE THE CRITERIA FOR AUTHENTICITY?

Subculturists combine a variety of criteria to construct and measure authenticity. For example, in evaluating authenticity, subculturists make several comparisons: between their group and outsiders; between the current scene and its past; and between old and new participants (Widdicombe and Wooffitt 1990). Sociologist Howard Becker's (1963) classic study of jazz showed how musicians positioned themselves as "hip" compared to more "square," main-stream non-musicians. Additionally, the criteria below often figure into authenticity work. Remember, the following are not *objective* standards but rather a sampling of statuses and principles to which subculturists commonly give special meaning.

OLD SCHOOL AND UNDERGROUND

Subculturists, especially those connected with music scenes, often venerate "the underground," disdaining prefabricated music or and mass-produced styles perceived as being created primarily to make money. Music producers have for decades manufactured "boy bands": New Kids on the Block, 'N Sync, Boyz II Men, New Edition, Backstreet Boys. For 30 years a string of young men performed with Puerto Rican boy band Menudo, rotating out when their voices changed or they lost their boyish looks. This rational, instrumental approach to making music (and an image) contrasts with a spontaneous, artistic, original creativity presumed to flourish in underground music. Underground musicians purportedly play for the "right" reasons; in other words, for the creative expression, meaningful relationships, and joy of the experience rather than for fame or money. Of course many poor, struggling "underground" musicians' goal *is* to get paid! But fans at least *perceive* their commercial goals as secondary to their artistic integrity.

Subculturists also often honor people and practices seen as close to the perceived emergence of the "original" subculture, the "old school." Thus mixed martial arts trainers and fighters with connections to the famed Gracie family – creators of Brazilian jiu-jitsu – automatically gain prestige with many fighters. Likewise, many in the fetish, BDSM, and body modification subcultures look to Fakir Musafar, father of the modern primitive movement, for inspiration; to have attended his early workshops and studied his philosophy would gain subcultural cache. Even **geography** often has some bearing on authenticity claims. Is Mississippi blues or Chicago blues more authentic? (Even in Mississippi there are distinctions between *delta* blues and *hill country* blues.) Can "real" anime come from anywhere but Japan? In some cases, insiders most value local knowledge and proximity to "sacred" or "original" subcultural spaces; in other cases, more cosmopolitan experience is revered.

GENDER, RACE, CLASS, AND AGE

Gender is often another criteria of authenticity. In many sub-cultures, men have a clear advantage when it comes to being perceived as authentic adherents. Participants assume they are "natural" participants, present for their love of the subcultural experience. Even avowedly gender-neutral subcultures with many women such as goth provide men greater access to authenticity and status (Brill 2007). Women often have more to prove, as some scenesters assume women participate only due to some connection to a man – "she's so-and-so's girlfriend." Ben Hutcherson and my work on extreme metal shows that entire subgenres of music emerge in part as gendered attempts at authenticity (Hutcherson and Haenfler 2010). The most sonically and topically extreme, most "brutal" metal gained popularity in the midst of the more feminine glam rock scene and many participants continue to juxtapose their "aggressive" music against "softer" fare.

Race is yet another factor around which subculturists build authenticity. Can a white musician play the blues? In his study of the Chicago blues scene, David Grazian (2003: 13) notes that on the "sliding scale of authenticity" black bluesmen from Chicago's South Side are considered the most authentic. White blues musicians must pay homage to black bluesmen without blatantly mimicking (or appropriating) their style. Some blues fans simply reject the notion that a young white man can *really* play the blues, while others are more accepting if he has had a hard life or is somehow connected to a black bluesman (Dessier 2006). Complicating matters further, blues club owners draw upon and reinforce stereotypes of black men and women as they cater to audiences' (and tourists') expectations. White audiences, in search of an authentic experience of music with "soul," only want to see black musicians, seeking the "real deal" regardless, to an extent, of musical skill or stage presence (Grazian 2003). (This process also partly explains the explosion of "gangsta rap" in the 1990s, as white consumers demanded a very specific, stereotypical, and narrow, performance of blackness.) Again, authenticity is a *social* process over which a particular subculturist does not have complete control.

CAN WHITE PEOPLE RAP?

Debates around "authentic" hip hop often revolve around whether white emcees and fans are "privileged interlopers" or evidence of hip hop's power to bridge racial divides. Some argue that the "black experience" is essential to hip hop. Others argue that claiming hip hop is a "black" culture reinforces the idea that there is some essential "blackness" or universal "black culture," while also concealing the experiences of hip hop kids who fit into neither black nor white categories (see Harrison 2008). Grazian (2003: 41) sums up the feelings of many black writers and artists: "authenticity claims rooted in notions of racial difference all too often reinforce traditional racial stereotypes of rhythmic and uncivilized blacks who radically differ from their white counterparts." Just as subculturists (and others) can attempt to reinforce race-based authenticity, so too can they disrupt essentialist notions of race by disconnecting authenticity from racial categories. Hip hop simultaneously exposes whiteness by constructing black emcees as the norm while creating a multiracial environment in which old essentializing beliefs don't hold up. Aware that their whiteness (and their privilege) has been exposed, many white emcees acknowledge their whiteness in the course of building their legitimacy. As Ian Maxwell (2003: 161) shows in a study of Australian hip hop, "it is okay to be white and into Hip Hop as long as you don't *misrepresent* who you are." White emcees must strive for authenticity without seeming to simply *appropriate* black cultural forms as so often happens. Eminem says this outright, comparing his use of black music (and its resulting wealth) to Elvis' taking of rock 'n' roll, and asserting that were he black he would have sold only half the records he did sell (Fraley 2009). Still, when white rappers insist that hip hop is "colorblind" as a means to reinforce their authenticity, they fall back on their white privilege and risk minimizing racial discrimination.

In addition to gender and race, **social class** often becomes a significant marker of authenticity. As many musicians and artists can attest, financial success can spark charges of selling out. Blues musicians, for example, are supposed to be poor, playing in small, dingy juke joints music that reflects their and their audiences' experience as struggling African Americans. Mississippi bluesman R. L. Burnside was the "real deal" because his music reflected his hardscrabble life – he *lived* the blues and epitomized the dangerous bluesman who sold his soul to the devil in exchange for musical talent. This image was at least in part cultivated by record labels, the media, and even fans. Being financially successful is not inherently damning. Rather, the perception that such success comes from catering to white middle-class audiences raises suspicions of selling out (Dessier 2006).

Some middle-class subcultures appropriate practices deemed working-class (even "trashy") for ironic purposes. Contemporary hipsters are known for drinking the cheap, unpretentious Pabst Blue Ribbon beer, largely considered a blue collar beer (see text box below). Likewise, ironic mesh caps featuring NASCAR logos creates a symbolic distance from bourgeoisie tastes even while reinforcing the idea that hobbies and interests associated with the working-class are silly or lowbrow. Type and quality of tattoo may suggest different meanings depending upon context. As sociologist Katie Irwin suggests:

> [Middle-class tattooees] like to play with fringe identities without sacrificing their middle class status. They get a tattoo that is thumbing their nose at middle class society in a way that is so mainstream that it would be hard to push them out.
>
> (in Rohrer 2007)

Age can work for and against the performance of authenticity (Mullaney 2012). Younger scenesters may dismiss "old" participants who inappropriately hang on to their youth, failing to merge their subcultural passions with "adult" achievements of home, work, and family (Davis 2006) (more on this in Chapter 8). The 45-year-old club "kid" who eschews full-time work in favor of rolling on ecstasy and dancing until 5am every weekend (while dressed in neon!) might be judged negatively. In some scenes, ageing correlates with a change in participation as, for example, older participants congregate at the back of a venue while younger ones mosh near the stage (Fonorow 2006). Less willing or able to take part in the authenticity rituals, older participants may be perceived by their youthful counterparts as less authentic. (Of course those same "older" participants have their own interpretation, focused more on *being* subcultural rather than *doing* a subcultural performance!)

Somewhat related to age, subculturists typically value some degree of **consistency**. For example, Ian MacKaye, progenitor of the straight edge movement, still maintains a drug-free, cruelty-free lifestyle even as he enters his fifth decade. Crudely put, subculturists tend to look down upon those whose involvement they perceive as temporary, as following a trend. Less committed to subcultural values, such "tourists" practice a deviance of convenience, safely participating with little long-term commitment or sacrifice. However, post-subculture theory suggests that impermanence pervades some scenes, perhaps making consistency less important.

While identifying the patterns in subcultural authenticity described above may seem easy enough, the more important insight is that values, identities, styles, and practices take on symbolic meaning in the context of ongoing interactions among subculturists themselves. These meanings may have some stability and may even span scenes, but subculturists also contest their authenticity and downplay their significance.

SUBCULTURAL CAPITAL: DO YOU HAVE THE RIGHT STUFF?

Each of these criteria amounts to what Sarah Thornton (1995) calls **subcultural capital**, including the objects, practices, and beliefs that subculturists use to distinguish themselves from outsiders and to demonstrate authenticity to insiders. Thornton builds upon the work of Pierre Bourdieu (1984) who discusses several types of capital, including *cultural* capital used to distinguish oneself from others and project a certain image. In certain circles, a designer handbag sends a message that one has taste and wealth, while knowledge of the opera signals refinement and class. Subculturists may use different, less "mainstream" objects to symbolize status, but they do so nonetheless. Thornton suggests they strive to be (and to be *seen* to be) "in the know," listening to the coolest underground music, wearing the right clothes, sporting the latest hairstyle, and knowing the moves to the latest dances (Thornton 1995: 11–12). Subcultural capital is situational, its meanings emerging via interaction in a given context. Subculturists walk a fine line between displaying esoteric knowledge and owning the "right" merch and being perceived as overdoing it: "Keeping the scene alive or supporting the scene, such as buying records or attending shows, are positively evaluated. *Being* scene/seen, however, is not" (Force 2009: 301). Further, they may mock the authenticity game even as they play it, joking about earning "scene points" or being a "scenester."

Specialized knowledge is a common sort of (sub)cultural capital. Hackers, such as those in the Anonymous collective, value particularly clever, funny, or difficult hacks against targets such as the police (see Haenfler 2012c). Knowing the "right" music and venues and the minutia of subcultural history can raise one's status. As you can imagine, owning (and strategically displaying) the right "stuff" is also an important aspect of subcultural capital. Record collections, cars, and motorbikes all become **sacred objects** in their respective scenes. For bike messengers, fixed gear (or track) bikes symbolize skill and daring, while for steampunks an especially original, well-crafted clockwork device captures their anachronistic fantasy. Hipsterism isn't confined to North America and Western Europe, as Russian youth seek out "ironic-glamour" clothing, frequent the "right" cafes, galleries, and bookstores, and are current with the latest music, books, and films meaningful within their social circles (Novikova 2011).

Our **bodies** can become an important source of subcultural capital and a way to perform authenticity, specifically via body modifications, fashion/style (see the Your Scene Sucks site at the end of this chapter), physique, and body performance (e.g. dancing) (see Driver 2011a). **Body modifications** such as tattoos and piercings are layered with meaning, and even basic **physique** can serve as subcultural capital. Suicide Girls must balance a youthful, slender body that meets many of the socially defined standards of beauty with enough *defiance* of mainstream beauty norms to set them apart from fashion models. Thus tattoos, piercings, and fluorescent hair cut in alternative styles situates the Suicide Girls as more "real" than women who pose in the *Sports Illustrated* "swimsuit" issue. **Fashion** and **style** compose a significant marker of authenticity in many scenes. The right clothes can signify belonging, although too much focus on fashion is often a faux pas. More radical styles can symbolize greater commitment. Just as important, however, are the ways subculturists deploy their style. A goth who dresses the part regardless of context – at work or in public – may claim greater authenticity than part-time subcultural "tourists." "Hardcore" punks live the subculture's ideals more thoroughly and consistently, while "preppie" punks and spectators dabble (Fox 1987). In contrast, studying the Australian hardcore scene, Chris Driver (2011a) found that style *was not* important to participants' evaluations of authenticity. Participants evaluated and experienced embodied authenticity in *practical* rather than *symbolic* terms, primarily knowing and correctly performing dance moves in the context of a hardcore show. While moshing may seem chaotic and undisciplined to an outsider, hardcore kids insisted it was not something anyone could "just do." Only by consistently *doing* could they develop the **body competency** necessary to successfully mosh. Beyond a cognitive understanding of moshing, such competency is *felt*, evoking certain emotions. It is "knowledge internalised in the realisation of sensory experience" (Driver 2011a), as much about affect and emotion as it is carefully considered technique. Finally, **body performance** is especially vital to b-boys and b-girls as they dance, and skaters and traceurs use their bodies to build subcultural capital via landing the most difficult tricks. They, like Driver's hardcore kids, develop skill and "rhythmic fluency" as they achieve "synergy between the body and the ecology" (Driver 2011a).

COMMERCIALIZATION AND COMMODIFICATION: WHERE DO SUBCULTURES GO TO DIE?

Always on the lookout for how to better exploit the lucrative youth market, entrepreneurs of all kinds look to subcultures for the next cool thing. "Edgy" countercultures, properly packaged, turn into corporate slogans, as when Nike used the Beatles anthem "Revolution" to sell shoes (Frank 1998). Subculturists, like others, are consumers, distinguishing themselves from others in part by what they buy (and *don't* buy). The CCCS scholars recognized this and Dick Hebdige (1979) saw commodification as the death knell of punk. Recall from Chapter 1 that some post-subculturists take this argument a step further, arguing that subcultures are defined *primarily* by their consumption. Are subculturists in some ways dupes of the corporate culture industry? Are they not only buying into test-marketed, off-the-rack styles but also prefabricated *identities*?

Theodor Adorno and other critical theorists sharply criticized popular culture for turning citizens into docile, passive consumers who pursue vacant pleasures instead of struggling against repressive economic/political systems (Adorno 1991; Friedman 1981). The "**culture industry**" encompasses the corporate controlled media industry (e.g. film studios and TV networks) focused on profitability rather than creativity, upholding a consumerist status quo rather than presenting a diversity of challenging ideas. The shallow content is meant to reach as broad an audience as possible, producing a **mass culture** that is at once phony and pacifying. Knowing that people want to *feel* like individuals, the culture industry markets what are essentially variations on the same stuff while producing what Adorno called **pseudo individualization**, a "fake" individualism in which we believe we have individual taste and free choice but in fact are consuming formulaic popular culture. Is one reality television show really so different from another? In championing individual expression, subcultures seemingly challenge mass culture. Yet subcultural styles, symbols, and practices quickly become commodities – and may have always been so.

PABST GETS HIP

Pabst Blue Ribbon (or PBR as its fans know it) has become the beer of choice for many subculturists. Just how did Pabst Blue Ribbon become a staple in the hipster scene? Maybe because it's cheap? Perhaps in part, but there are cheaper beers. Pabst sales were hitting rock bottom in the early 2000s until alternative urbanites in Portland, Oregon, took it up because its scarcity and lack of advertising – and therefore lack of image – contrasted it with bigger, ubiquitous brands such as Miller and Coors. Pabst seemed like an underground beer, a "working man's" beer, offering a symbolic thumb in the eye to corporate culture and to Portland's microbrew crowd alike. Naturally, the company went to work decoding its newfound popularity. Recognizing young people's backlash against advertising, Pabst marketers have kept their marketing subtle – no celebrity endorsements, no TV ads, no ads on rock radio stations. Instead, when asked, Pabst sponsors bike messenger events, skateboarding film screenings, art openings, and other small events. An internal market analysis suggests that being the beer of punks, ska-ters, and other misfits is good business, marking Pabst the brand of social protest, of "lifestyle as dissent." Yet the business must expand – punks and indie rockers are not enough. The conclusion: try to sell a lot of beer without becoming too trendy, to develop brand loyalty without treating Pabst loyalists as a marketing niche. What does the future of Pabst hold? Who knows, but rest assured that marketers are keeping careful watch.

(Walker 2003)

Corporate marketers have long sought to capitalize on subcultural "cool," deliberately transforming subversive scenes into marketing niches. Consider the case of Harley-Davidson motorcycle enthusiasts. Harley motorcycles, especially, represent *freedom*, a way to trade the predictability and order of mundane life for the immediate, sensual pleasures of the open road (Primm 2004; Hopper and Moore 1983). Classic films such as *The Wild One* (1953) and *Easy Rider* (1969) depict young bikers as outsiders and rebels. Beyond freedom, *outlaw* motorcycle clubs represented anarchy and mayhem, a resounding rejection of conformist culture reinforced by a killing involving the Hells Angels at the 1969 Altamont Free Concert in California. Yet behind the scenes of the seemingly rebellious biker subculture oper-ate a host of businesspeople seeking to boost profitability while maintaining the Harley "mystique," as one study suggests:

For firms that sell a mystique as well as a hard product, understanding and managing the mystique may be critical to long-term profitability. Likely, the management of mystique has direct implications for issues such as licensing, brand equity and promotion. For example, the mar-keter must consider trade-offs between short-term gains through brand extensions, and the potential dilution or debilitation of the mystique associated with the core brand or product.

(Schouten and McAlexander 1993: 392)

The study's authors recognized that Harley needed to cultivate the appeal of bikers' "dangerous" or deviant image without becoming over-associated with outlaw gangs:

Another trade-off to be considered lies between identification with and renunciation of deviant aspects of the core subculture. Harley-Davidson has successfully borrowed from outlaw biker symbolism while balancing the deviance inherent in that association with such wholesome activities as rider safety seminars and family and children's activities at company sponsored rallies.

(Schouten and McAlexander 1993: 392)

While subculturists may sneer at the commodification of their scene and idealize its less commercial past, many seemingly "underground" scenes had commercial intentions at their inception. Malcolm McLaren and Vivienne Westwood ran a London boutique catering to mods and punks, and McLaren created the Sex Pistols with commercial intentions (Savage 2002). Likewise, Sylvia Robinson assembled the Sugarhill Gang to cut rap's first commercially successful record, "Rapper's Delight," intending to market and sell a lot of records (and succeeding) (Watkins 2005). So while commercialization may be a matter of degree, to lament the demise of a non-commercial underground is to engage in a bit of revisionist history.

MARKETING AND SUBCULTURES

- Tokidoki makes a tattooed Barbie doll complete with pink hair, funky handbag, and even neck tattoos.
- A variety of graffiti art coloring books allow kids to "create" street-style art in the safety of their home.
- São Paulo, Brazil, features an entire mall devoted to heavy metal called Grandes Galerias. Brazilian thrash metal legends Sepultura appeared in a 2008 Volkswagen advertisement.

DIFFUSION AND DEFUSION: WHAT HAPPENS TO SUBCULTURES OVER TIME?

The opening and closing ceremonies of the 2012 summer Olympic Games, held in London, featured a variety of British pop songs showcasing 50 years of the country's musical talent. In addition to radio friendly tunes by Duran Duran and The Beatles, the Sex Pistols' "Pretty Vacant" blared through the stadium as strange human/puppet hybrids pogo danced and leather-clad punks performed a choreographed routine. The band considered scandalous 35 years before for mocking the queen – "God save the queen, she ain't no human being!" – had been absorbed into Britain's cultural legacy alongside the Rolling Stones and The Who.

Despite, or perhaps because of, the negative attention many subcultures receive, some expand far beyond their initial emergence, eventually becoming part of the cultural lexicon. **Diffusion** occurs as subcultural symbols, objects, and practices spread beyond their original scene (Clarke 1976) (more on this in Chapter 7). Tattoos, for example, transcended the boundaries of any particular scene long ago, as seemingly every athlete, musician, and actor has multiple tattoos (not to mention many doctors, lawyers, and professors). As many societies become more culturally diverse and as the internet accelerates the spread of ideas and trends, nothing stays underground for long. Increasingly mobile, heterogeneous societies may not react to some subcultures *at all* except, perhaps, as marketing niches.

As celebrities, "normals," and trendy boutiques appropriate subcultural styles, their potential for resistance declines. Diffusion often leads to **defusion**, wherein subcultures lose their shock value, their resistance potential, and become marketing tools (although some would argue they were never anything more in the first place!). Hot Topic, a chain of more than 600 suburban North American alternative fashion stores, markets "alternative" clothing, toys, and other trinkets inspired by the goth, emo, skater, and metal scenes. Skateboarding and other "extreme" sports have spawned the X-Games and other corporate competitions. Likewise, parkour competitions have sprung up around the world, some of which fabricate obstacle environments indoors. Even the Burning Man festival's utopian vision has come under siege as its popularity forces organizers to more rationally plan and control the event, addressing government regulations, camp safety, and environmental concerns.

Commercialization also shapes authenticity claims related to race. Arguments about hip hop's "blackness" revolve mainly around rap music; Latinos (and others) have long had a more visible role in DJing, graffiti, and b-boying. As it is the most commercially viable (by far) of all hip hop elements, the stakes surrounding rap music's authenticity are great; in contrast, there is little popular debate regarding *racial* authenticity of graffiti-writers (Harrison 2008).

RESISTANCE VS. INCORPORATION

Dick Hebdige (1979) describes two forms of **incorporation**, or ways subcultures become woven into the mainstream, thereby reducing their threat. The first, **ideological incorporation**, occurs when cultural or political authorities make light of subcultures, often reducing them to their spectacular styles and lampooning their outlandish behaviors. The second, **commodity incorporation**, involves mass marketing subcultural styles, symbols, and music, as the chain of Hot Topic stores has done so effectively in the US. In robbing subcultures of their exclusivity and subversive purpose, or reducing them to mass-produced styles, they become trivial, less upsetting.

Arguments that contemporary subcultures are pale, even meaningless imitations of their original incarnations obscure the fact that subculturists are present to, aware of, and often resistant to commodification. Faced with incorporation, some subculturists "circle the wagons" to protect their subcultural capital, labeling anyone who misuses (by their rationale) subcultural styles, practices, and ideals as "sell-outs" and "poseurs" (Moore 2005). Threatened with assimilation in the 1990s as hip hop exploded on the radio and MTV, artists more fervently inserted authenticity claims into their music that reflect the criteria I previously discussed. They feared that major labels, white rappers, and advertising executives might misrepresent or even *erase* hip hop's African American roots. Via lyrics and media interviews they insisted that "real" rap is black (race), hard (gender/sexuality), from the underground and the street (geography), respects the "old school" (age, longevity), and is about staying true to yourself (consistency) (McLeod 1999). Thus white rappers House of Pain and even black rapper-turned-movie-star Will Smith faced accusations of being fake because of their massive popularity with suburban white audiences.

Other subculturists seek new avenues in which to *take back* their scene from profiteers. Riot grrrls, for instance, recognized how quickly popular musicians such as the Spice Girls appropriated their "grrrl" power slogan and how fast "girl" power became just another marketing device (Jacques 2001; Schilt 2003). Across their 20-year history, riot grrrls have **reappropriated** girl power by forming *new* (less- or non-commercial) spaces of resistance such as online 'zines, feminist music festivals, and even rock camps for girls, in which young women spend a week learning to play rock instruments (Giffort 2012). Commodification also sparks new subcultural innovation, motivating underground participants to both return to the scene's "roots" and to make their own mark (Haenfler 2006). Punk may have died several deaths since 1977, but crust punks around the world still make politically and aesthetically challenging music and while living their lives by a radical DIY code. Big business tried to turn riot grrrls back into cultural *consumers*, but in line with the movement's original intention, rock camps encourage young women to be cultural *producers*.

KEY INSIGHTS

- Pursuing, performing, and judging authenticity is central to most subcultural experience, despite many subculturists' claims of being above such petty concerns. However, authenticity is not an achievement but rather an ongoing negotiation.
- There is no "objective" measure of authenticity. Rather, people construct the meanings, criteria, and importance of authenticity in the context of particular social settings and relationships.
- The so-called "original" incarnations of a subculture are not automatically more authentic. Many have commercial roots, many contemporary participants actively resist incorporation, and age and originality are simply criteria of authenticity deployed and given meaning by subculturists.
- Subcultures nearly always have some commercial aspect, although some subculturists attempt to operate primarily in smaller-scale subcultural economies. Still, in the past 20 years corporate profiteers have become ever more sophisticated in appropriating from subcultures, mining the "underground" for potentially profitable ideas and styles.
- Rather than "killing" subcultures, commodification often inspires new subcultural innovations.

EXPLORING FURTHER

Blue Chicago: The Search for Authenticity in Urban Blues Clubs, by David Grazian, 2003 (University of Chicago Press). An intimate examination of the lives of blues musicians and fans and how they construct authenticity.

"Racial Authenticity in Rap Music and Hip Hop," by Anthony Kwame Harrison, 2008 (*Sociology Compass* 2(6): 1783–1800). A thorough overview of the scholarship related to racial authenticity in hip hop.

Authenticity in Culture, Self, and Society, edited by Philip Vannini and J. Patrick Williams, 2009 (Ashgate). This volume offers a variety of perspectives on the concept of authenticity.

Dust & Illusions: 30 Years of History of Burning Man, directed by Olivier Bonin, 2009. A documentary following the transformation of the Burning Man festival from a small, subversive experiment in community to a large, regulated, organized event. You can watch the film for free at dustandillusions.com.

The Steampunk World's Fair, http://steampunkworldsfair.com. A trove of information about steampunk.

Your Scene Sucks, www.yourscenesucks.com. This site (and book) offers hilarious satirical profiles of an array of scenesters, from "fixed gear hipster" and "generic emo girl" to "crustpunk" and "juggaloo clown." Each profile features a fashion analysis, playlist, and a brief description. Useful for thinking about the performative nature of authenticity.

6

HOW DOES SOCIETY REACT TO SUBCULTURES?

In the 1970s, sociologist William J. Chambliss studied two groups of high school boys in a Seattle suburb, following their exploits for two years while making careful field observations. One group, which Chambliss labeled the "Saints," were popular, well-dressed, middle-class kids who drove nice cars, played sports, and received good grades. Their counterparts – the "Roughnecks" – were lower class boys, more known for their habitual fighting (mostly among themselves) than for their success in school. *Both* groups of boys regularly caused trouble, skipping school, engaging in petty theft, and drinking alcohol. Yet the Roughnecks received far more attention from the police and other authorities, while community members saw the Saints as good boys who occasionally engaged in relatively harmless pranks. It's not that the Saints were any less delinquent; they drove while drunk, engaged in vandalism, cheated on exams, and even played jokes on the police. In fact, Chambliss found that the Saints committed *more* delinquent acts than the Roughnecks – they had greater access to alcohol and automobiles and were able to more easily concoct reasons to skip school. However, the Roughnecks received greater scrutiny and faced much harsher punishment for their behavior. The Saints' deviance was less visible, they were more savvy about how to politely talk their way out of trouble with the police, and, significantly, the community saw them as upstanding young men with bright futures. Chambliss (1973) wrote: "Those in low places, like the Roughnecks, are much more likely to be arrested and imprisoned while people in high places, like the Saints, usually avoid paying such a high price for their crimes." Chambliss's study illustrates that community reaction to subcultures hinges less on the actual deviant behavior and more on the "offender's" social status or how he or she is labeled. In this case, social class and the power and reputation it conferred benefited the Saints (the "good kids") and worked against the Roughnecks (the "troublemakers").

As I discussed in Chapter 5, many subcultures increasingly occupy a "normal" space in conventional society, evoking little response at all. Many subcultural styles and practices eventually make their way into popular culture, losing their "shock value" as they become increasingly commodified. Nevertheless, subcultures continue to provoke disproportionately negative responses from more conventional circles. In this chapter, I explore the relationship between subcultures and their "parent" societies – how do societies react to subcultures? Politicians, law enforcement, religious leaders, parents, school administrators and other authorities often respond to subculturists with suspicion, moral judgment, or even fear. I examine how moral entrepreneurs wage crusades against subcultural groups they view as a threat, fuelling moral panics that justify monitoring or even persecuting subculturists.

MORAL PANIC: ARE SUBCULTURES "DANGEROUS?"

Outsiders often perceive "strange" groups not just as oddities but as threats, giving rise to the belief that subcultures are dangerous. Periodically, tragic events seem to bear these fears out. On April 20, 1999, two young men brought a variety of firearms into Columbine High School near Littleton, Colorado, killing 12 students, one teacher, and themselves. The media reported the killers' interest in violent video games and films, heavy metal music, and (erroneously) goth culture, painting the duo as weird, troubled youths. Officials mistakenly identified the boys with a small clique known as the "Trenchcoat Mafia," a group of gamers who wore trenchcoats but had little connection to the killers, suggesting that the boys' subcultural affiliations may have motivated the massacre.

Their dark clothing, musical tastes, and interest in violent media intensified fears of subcultural youth, particularly goths. Administrators at schools across the US rushed to implement new school safety measures, including posting guards, installing metal detectors, and requiring that students use transparent backpacks. On the other side of the world, in June 2002, two Chinese boys, aged 13 and 14, burned down an unlicensed cyber café in Beijing after a dispute with staff members, killing 24 patrons and injuring another 13. Called the "Chinese Columbine" by media scholar Henry Jenkins (2002), the event sparked a government shutdown of internet cafés as officials claimed that online pornography, gambling, and video games amounted to "electric opium," presumably leading to addiction and anti-social behavior. The boys, both gamers, symbolized a mood that Chinese society was changing too fast, that youth were growing away from traditional cultural and political conventions. Finally, the media blamed horror films and anime for Japanese serial killer Tsutomu Miyazaki's grisly killings of young girls, calling him the "Otaku Murderer." In each of these cases, authorities cited youths' real or imagined subcultural affiliations as motivations for their crimes.

While such awful events rightfully inspire reflection, worry, and even policy changes, the media often incorrectly connect subcultures to such tragedies, exaggerating the danger, stigmatizing *all* subculturists, and generating a moral panic. A **moral panic** ensues when a significant number of people believe a group or practice threatens the social order or fundamental social ideals (Thompson 1998). Stanley Cohen outlined the basic pattern of moral panics in the classic text *Folk Devils and Moral Panics: The Creation of the Mods and the Rockers*:

> A condition, episode, person or group of persons emerges to become defined as a threat to societal values and interests; its nature is presented in a stylized and stereotypical fashion by the mass media; the moral barricades are manned by editors, bishops, politicians and other right-thinking people; socially accredited experts pronounce their diagnoses and solutions; ways of coping are evolved or (more often) resorted to; the condition then disappears, submerges or deteriorates and becomes more visible.

> (Cohen 2002 [1972]: 9)

Cohen developed his theory in the context of a media furor around the Bank Holiday riots of 1964–1966 in which gatherings of young people, including subcultural youth such as mods and rockers, fought, broke shop windows, and rode their scooters and motorbikes up and down the streets of several seaside resort towns. While violence certainly occurred, Cohen argued the media sensationalized and exaggerated the "danger," making "mods" a symbol for any youthful threat to the moral order.

The potential for and significance of a moral panic depends in large part on the social and political context in which deviance occurs. In both Singapore and Malaysia heavy metal provoked a degree of moral outrage. In Singapore, the resulting panic was tempered by government secularism and restrictions against allegations of satanism. In Malaysia, however, religious leaders effectively framed black metal as anti-Islamic, based upon stories of metalheads burning the Quran (Liew and Fu 2006). In both countries, political parties and religious leaders competed to be the moral protectors of youth, projecting local fears onto the metalheads. However, the traction such demonization gained depended upon the national context; Singapore's secularism and small Christian and Islamic communities muted the effect of satanic panics.

HOW CAN WE TELL IF SOMETHING IS A MORAL PANIC OR A GENUINE THREAT?

To a certain degree, the danger of subcultural activities is in the eye of the beholder; what one person deems a moral threat another sees as a benign lifestyle choice. Of course some subcultures *are* dangerous. Racist skinhead gangs and football hooligan firms *do* occasionally create mayhem. BASE jumping crews that parachute from buildings and bridges pursue an illegal, potentially dangerous pastime. Graffiti artists *do* perpetrate often-unwanted defacing of property. The "one-percenters" of motorcycle clubs, better known as outlaw motorcycle gangs, *do* engage in violence, drug-dealing, and other crime. So how do we tell when members of society are guarding against a genuine threat versus promoting a moral panic?

First, let's remind ourselves that just as *subculture* is a concept and not a real "thing," so too does the concept of *moral panic* describe a range of ideas, beliefs, and social processes and relationships rather than some objectively observable phenomenon. Still, several general themes reoccur in case studies of the reactions to deviance: **concern**, **hostility**, **consensus**, **disproportionality**, and **volatility** (Goode and Ben-Yahuda 1994: 33–41). Moral panics typically begin with a growing **concern** about a group or behavior that may not reach the level of *fear* but indicates the perception of a threat. Concern is accompanied by **hostility**, usually from a specific group or part of society, towards those engaged in the deviant behavior or thought responsible for a perceived social problem (e.g. conservatives frequently blame gay and lesbian people for disrupting "traditional family values"). In the process, the "righteous" distinguish themselves from the "evil-doers." Cultural authorities oversimplify a problem (such as school violence), portraying the offending group as **folk devils** (such as goths). Folk devils symbolize the greater moral panic, caricatures that remind people of right and wrong and provide an easily recognizable target for exclusion, suppression, or reform. Subculturists often serve as excellent folk devils given their unorthodox beliefs, behaviors, and appearances. Male athletes perpetrate sexual assault and fraternity brothers consume alcohol at higher rates than the general population, yet public reaction rarely condemns the whole group or attributes such behavior to group membership. Social legitimacy serves as a cloak of protection for upstanding, high status groups. While not everyone in a given society accepts (and some actually oppose) the designation of a particular moral threat, enough **consensus** exists that the perception is relatively widespread. In other words, a moral panic is a form of *collective* behavior rather than individual prejudice.

To qualify as a moral panic, people's fear must be **out of proportion** to the actual threat. Of course the "reality" of a threat can be difficult to gauge, but we can empirically measure the supposed harm suggested by many moral panics, from crime rates to suicide. Some threats are completely baseless, as in the case of satanic ritual abuse in US daycare centers, of which no evidence exists (Bartholomew and Goode 2000). Others have some element of truth, but exaggerate the extent and degree of the danger. Consider the case of ecstasy use at raves, a problem that gained international attention in the 1990s. Although millions of youth attended raves and many, if not most, used ecstasy at some point, very few died as a result, and those few deaths are attributable more to dehydration and the context in which the ecstasy is used rather than to the drug per se (Thompson 1998).

Some scholars suggest that we fear the *wrong* things (Glassner 2010); there is little doubt, for example, that alcohol and other legal drugs kill exponentially more people than illegal drugs. Likewise, if we wish to protect children we might focus our efforts more on promoting seatbelts and bicycle helmets than requiring school uniforms and installing metal detectors in schools; accidents kill more kids than school shooters and are significantly more preventable.

Finally, moral panics entail a degree of **volatility**, meaning they often emerge quite suddenly and subside nearly as quickly (Goode and Ben-Yehuda 2009). Even panics that seem to persist for decades – such as the drug panic in the US – wax and wane, often shifting focus as new "threats" emerge (e.g. marijuana in the 1930s, LSD in the 1960s, ecstasy in the 1990s). The "satanic panics" of the 1980s emerged quickly (although certainly they have historical precedents) but had virtually disappeared by the mid-1990s (Victor 1993). Some panics simply fade away as circumstances change or authorities divert their attention to different problems – violence between mods and rockers declined as youth moved on to other scenes and adults grew worried about hippies and the counter-culture. Other panics result in ongoing scrutiny, public debate, and policy changes or even morph into social movements or professional lobbying organizations as in the case of fundamentalist Christians or the National Rifle Association in the US. Rarely, if ever, does a moral panic grip an entire society; while "mass hysteria" might make for thrilling cinema, it seldom occurs in real life.

While moral panics might not reach the level of mass hysteria, they are often extremely **emotionally charged** as people believe their fundamental values and ways of life are at stake. This is perhaps even more so in the case of subcultures, which commonly link to children or youth. Take the case of satanic ritual abuse in Canada, the US, Australia, and the UK, wherein social workers, therapists, law enforcement, religious leaders, and significant segments of the general public believed that satanic cults, practitioners of witchcraft, and diabolical daycare centers were sexually molesting and killing children as part of occult rituals. Scholars uncovered virtually no evidence to support such claims (La Fontaine 1998), yet because the allegations involved children and threatened dominant religious beliefs, emotions ran high with even well-meaning people believing rather outlandish claims.

In sum, "What is important is that the concern locates a 'folk devil,' is shared, is out of synch with the measurable seriousness of the condition that generates it, and varies in intensity over time" (Goode and Ben-Yahuda 1994: 41). While moral panics vary in duration and intensity and differ across cultures, they are one of most prevalent reactions to subcultures across the world.

MORAL ENTREPRENEURIAL CAMPAIGNS: WHO FUELS THE PANIC?

In some ways, moral entrepreneurial campaign is simply another way of describing a moral panic. "Panic," however, implies randomness, spontaneity, chaos, and chance, making a moral panic something that "just happened," as if there were no human beings with particular interests and intentions involved. On the contrary, **moral entrepreneurial campaign**, or **moral crusade**, suggests that real people strategically use power to shape a particular version of reality in service of their own agenda. Likewise, "campaign" or "crusade" captures the ongoing nature of moral panics and that such events unfold in stages (though not in discreet, linear steps).

Moral crusades originate from a variety of sources (Goode and Ben-Yahuda 1994). Some emerge at a **grassroots** level, when the general public fosters a genuine (if often ill-informed) concern, as in the case of street crime or drug abuse. Political **elites** may also generate moral panics, such as when right-leaning politicians in Europe and the US target immigrant populations in efforts to garner votes and pass restrictive legislation. Finally, **interest groups** such as social movements and nonprofit organizations promote moral panics, such as temperance movements that brand alcoholic beverages as sinful and socially destructive, in some cases successfully outlawing alcoholic beverages for a time. A nation's cultural climate and political structure influence the form and prevalence of moral panics (Critcher 2003). In more religious nations, moral entrepreneurs (see below) often emerge from the clergy, for example. In nations with less centralized political, legal, and media systems (e.g. the US as compared to the UK) panics more commonly begin locally, rather than from central political institutions, and eventually spread to the national level (Jenkins 1992; Critcher 2003).

DANGER: EMO IN MEXICO, IRAQ, SAUDI ARABIA, AND RUSSIA

Sometimes subculturists get caught up in broader moral crusades. In Iraq and Mexico, violence against "emo" youth coincides with anti-gay sentiment. Widely perceived as gay, emos have faced beatings in Mexico and murder by Iraqi militias (Grillo 2008). In Saudi Arabia, where most women wear the abaya cloak in public, religious police arrested ten women for wearing emo styles in a coffee shop (AFP Newswire 2010). Meanwhile, Russian lawmakers considered legislation that would regulate emo websites and ban emo and goth fashions in certain public buildings, believing the scene fosters depression and suicide (Michaels 2008).

MORAL ENTREPRENEURS

At whichever level moral crusades originate, at the forefront are **moral entrepreneurs**, "Groups or organizations [that] take it upon themselves to pronounce upon the nature of the problem and its best remedies" (Critcher 2003: 17). When metal band Metallica came to play my hometown of Rapid City, South Dakota in 1989, some community leaders tried to bar the band from playing, citing heavy metal's propensity to encourage sex, violence, and devil worship. Local ministers, acting as moral entrepreneurs, rallied the community against the band while the newspaper ran stories printing particularly offensive metal lyrics and questioning the genre's connections to the occult. Religious officials even managed to sway local police into issuing Metallica a warning to refrain from any "obscene" behavior. (They didn't.)

It may seem strange in hindsight that so many people are swayed by moral crusades. However, moral crusades often rest upon at least a grain of truth; many heavy metal bands do, after all, explore the macabre or the occult. More significantly, though, moral entrepreneurs strategically build legitimacy around their claims, relying upon **experts**, often with few or shady credentials, to bolster their cause. Heavy metal scares were not confined to the US. In 1991, authorities blamed metal, and Metallica in particular, in the death of a 15-year-old boy in Sydney, Australia. In 1987, Russian research-ers claimed that metal inhibited youths' work ethic as well as being addictive and physically harmful. Research psychologist G. Aminev explained:

> If [heavy metal listeners] are isolated from such music for a week their general level of health declines, they become more irritable, their hands start to tremble and their pulse becomes irregular. ... Some of them refused to continue with our experiments after the third day. This means we are witnessing a certain kind of illness. It seems that Rock music does not only have a psychological influence but a biochemical one too, for it seems connected with the appearance of the morphine-type sub-stances which induce 'pleasure'.
>
> (Walker 1987)

The ranks of moral entrepreneurs include politicians, law enforce-ment, religious leaders, and interest groups. **Politicians**, espe-cially, are in a position to be **rule creators**, those with the power to make new laws or regulations to eliminate the moral threat (Becker 1963). As I mentioned previously, as a result of the Columbine massacre, schools across the US installed metal detec-tors and required students to wear transparent backpacks, *despite* the fact that a Secret Service study suggested such physical safety efforts would be far less effective than listening to student warn-ings, intervening earlier in the potential shooter's planning pro-cess, and reducing bullying (Dedman 2000). Japanese lawmakers sought to regulate erotic content in films and books favored by Otaku as a result of the "Otaku Murderer" I mentioned above. **Law enforcement** regularly occupy the role of **rule enforcers**, implementing new laws, monitoring potential violators, and pun-ishing rule-breakers. In the US, the FBI have designated fans of "horrorcore" rap group Insane Clown Posse, called Juggalos, as a "gang threat": "Transient, criminal Juggalo groups pose a threat to communities due to the potential for violence, drug use/sales, and their general destructive and violent nature" (Federal Bureau of Investigation 2011). Such designations have real legal con-sequences for subculturists, increasing stigma and scrutiny, and compounding criminal penalties.

TIPPER GORE AND THE PMRC TAKE ON THE MUSIC INDUSTRY

It may sound ridiculous or seem funny in hindsight, but the 1980s were filled with seemingly dangerous music. The enemies? Metal bands such as Guns 'n' Roses, punk acts such as Jello Biafra, rap groups such as NWA ... even pop singers Cyndi Lauper, Frank Zappa, Prince, and John Denver. Tipper Gore, wife of then Senator Al Gore, led an organization called the Parent Music Resource Center to campaign against indecency and obscenity in music. With such political clout, this moral entrepreneurial campaign was able to encourage Congressional hearings on the dangers of music and gain widespread media coverage on news and talk shows such as *Oprah* and *Donahue*. *TIME* magazine featured a cover on filthy language in pop culture. Check out Jello debating Tipper in the video below.

YouTube: "Jello Biafra and Tipper Gore on Oprah,"
www.youtube.com/watch?v=L_SiOnt_Oxo

As I have suggested, **religious leaders** regularly play prominent roles in moral crusades as subculturists make excellent symbols of "evil" and moral crusades allow religious entrepreneurs the opportunity to "perform" (i.e. demonstrate) their righteousness. The late Reverend Jerry Falwell blamed feminists, pagans, gays, and other "secularists" for the September 11 terrorist attacks. Like their Christian counterparts, many Islamic leaders label heavy metal satanic (Levine 2009). Finally, non-religious **interest groups** use moral panics to lobby for new rules or capitalize upon existing crusades by offering their services to ameliorate the problem. For example, in the 1980s, The Parent Music Resource Center, led by Tipper Gore and other politicians' wives, convinced the US Congress to hold hearings investigating the damaging, anti-social influence of metal, rap, and other popular music, ultimately spurring the recording industry to place "Parental Advisory" stickers on records containing objectionable lyrics. Around the same time, the British Board of Film Censors (now *Classification*) banned certain horror films, dubbed "video nasties," from release on video cassette, in response to beliefs that such movies were morally depraved (Critcher 2003).

ACEH PUNKS

In late 2011, both state police and Sharia police arrested punks at a concert in Aceh province, Indonesia, detaining them for a week of "moral re-education" (Hasan 2011; Michaels and Johnson 2012). The deputy mayor called the concert "an abomination to Islamic teaching" and punks a threat to Islamic faith (Hasan and Hasan 2011). The mayor proposed sending the punks for psychological help and job training programs to better integrate the youths into society. So here we see religious leaders, politicians, law enforcement, and interest groups pooling their efforts to identify the moral threat, treat the punks as folk devils, and create and enforce rules.

THE MEDIA: ADDING FUEL TO THE MORAL PANIC FIRE?

Stanley Cohen emphasized the important role of the media in the creation of moral panics, especially at the outset of a crusade. Consider the following headline: "Anders Behring Breivik Trained for Mass Killing with Video Games *Call of Duty*, *World of Warcraft*" (Associated Press 2012). In 2011, right wing, ultra-nationalist, anti-Muslim Breivik killed 77 people in Norway to protest what he perceived as the country's liberal immigration and multicultural policies. The attention-grabbing headline implicates video games in the massacre under the guise of strictly reporting the "facts" – after all, Breivik claims he used games to train. Without further context, however, the implication is that gaming somehow *caused* or *played a significant role* in the killings, making gaming (and gamers) suspect. The media – newspapers, magazines, television news programs, websites, and blogs – can quickly transform sensational, but rare, events into patterns and even threats.

Cohen (2002 [1972]) identified three ways the media contributed to moral panics. First, the media **exaggerate** the extent or danger of the supposed threat and **distort** "facts" using sensational headlines or dramatic music during a news broadcast. Crime reality shows such as *To Catch a Predator* come to mind, giving the appearance that sexual predators are everywhere and seemingly "regular people" could be perpetrators. The media also often

predict that events will get worse without intervention, that problems are escalating. Taking everything the media says to heart, one might believe that drugs, serial killings, teen pregnancy, school shootings, and child abductions all consistently get worse. Finally, the media turn subculturists into caricatures, playing up the spectacular styles and bizarre rituals in a process of **symbolization**, thereby capturing the threat in an easily recognizable form (Cohen 1972, cited in Thompson 1998: 33). An *LA Times* article titled "The Twisted World of a 'Straight Edge' Gang" featured the tagline "Utah offshoot of anti-drug, animal-rights movement has mutated into a violent group of 'suburban terrorists'" (Sahagun 1998). While a minority of straight edge kids resemble the tattooed thugs described in the media, the vast majority live out the "positive" ethos their music espouses (Haenfler 2006). Applying Cohen's theory, the *label* "straight edge" became symbolic of a *status* (terrorist, gang member), and *objects* (the 'X' symbol, tattoos, piercings, straight edge band shirts) symbolized the label and status, tainting *all* straight edgers with a "violent" or "potential criminal" label.

The media play an important role in creating a **signification spiral** (Hall et al. 1978) which links various social problems (e.g. homosexuality and child abuse) while amplifying the perceived threat: "the interaction of claims-makers, moral entrepreneurs and the mass media results in the establishment of a discourse in which certain groups are demonized as the source of moral decline" (Thompson 1998: 31). News professionals do not simply report the "facts" surrounding events. Rather, they choose what to report (after all, there is too much potential news, even with a 24-hour news cycle) and how to report it (considering the presumed audience), often privileging stories the public finds bizarre, dramatic, emotional, or sensational. Thus when TV's *America's Most Wanted* paints straight edgers as radical animal rights terrorists, the media reduces the subculture to an easily digestible stereotype. Once the media (and others) repeat a story or theme enough, a "common sense" discourse prevails in which people take for granted that subculturists and other folk devils are problematic (Hall 1973). This may be especially true in the age of new media in which emails, Facebook posts, and Twitter feeds with wildly exaggerated claims can go viral in a matter of days. Media reports stereotyping or even demonizing subculturists thrive in societies where fear and risk interweave into daily life. Media scholar David Altheide (2002) suggests that more than being afraid of various, discreet social problems (crime, drugs, AIDS, etc.) some cultures create a general atmosphere of worry, even threat.

Sometimes the news media inadvertently helps to *create* the very reality they erroneously report. Consider the case of "satanic" Norwegian black metal. In the early 1990s, Mayhem vocalist Per Yngve "Dead" Ohlin killed himself, Emperor drummer Bård "Faust" Eithun was convicted of murder, and Burzum and Mayhem's Varg Vikernes killed fellow musician "Euronymous." Meanwhile, police implicated influential black metal musicians, including Vikernes, in a series of church burnings, including historic "stave" churches hundreds of years old. The press, understandably, thoroughly reported on these terrible crimes, quickly linking black metal to satanism. However, black metal initially centered much more on an anti-Christian message than actual satanic themes; Vikernes, for example, is better described as a pagan nationalist, wanting to restore Nordic people's "native" religion. Nevertheless, a sensationalist exposé of supposedly cultish satanists in the early 1990s provided Norwegian youth an image of "evil," and some black metal musicians and fans adopted its trappings, incorporating pentagrams and upended crucifixes into their fashion and satanic imagery into their lyrics (Moynihan and Søderlind 2003). Eventually, the reports linking black metal to satanism actually *increased* youth's exposure to and adoption of satanic motifs, strengthening the links between them. So-called satanic black metal thus owes much of its growth (such that it is) to media.

Subculturists alternately (and often simultaneously) despise and welcome media coverage (Thornton 1995). Negative media reports reinforce subculturists' outsider status, boosting their authenticity. And scenesters who make a living from the scene (e.g. musicians, promoters, shopkeepers) may appreciate the exposure. The media may also "create" subcultures by identifying, naming, and describing what we think of as subcultural activity (Thornton 1995), giving some semblance of order to previously unorganized and uncategorized behavior. Was there really an emo identity or scene prior to music journalists' widespread use of the term (see Azerrad 2001)? (And despite, I might add, opposition to the label from those it was used to describe.)

POWER AND POLITICS: WHY BOTHER WITH MORAL PANICS?

Even an understanding of how moral panics occur leaves us wondering *Why* would moral entrepreneurs take the time? What is the *point* of moral entrepreneurial campaigns? And how are moral entrepreneurs able to frame subculturists in such narrow terms? As I have shown, in the wake of moral panics, moral entrepreneurs and rule creators call for greater social control and a return to "traditional" values (Thompson 1998). Politicians can use a moral panic to gain support as was likely in the case of the crackdown on Aceh punks. In fact, governments regularly use moral panics about subcultures for their own political purposes, often **scapegoating** youth to gain votes and avoid confronting complex problems. Officials may blame graffiti-writers and street gangs for urban decline, avoiding the reality that deteriorating inner cities result from deindustrialization and its attendant problems, while disguising structural racism and government neglect. Likewise, after the 2005 riots in Paris, perpetrated primarily by young, marginalized immigrants from North Africa, 200 members of the French Parliament called for legal action against hip hop artists such as Monsieur R, claiming rappers incited youth to violence (BBC News 2005). While it is impossible to pinpoint exactly the causes of the riots, no doubt chronic high unemployment, racism, and a perception of police harassment contributed more to the conflict than rap music. In fact, musicians had been rapping about these very issues for years, yet life in the *banlieues* (low-income suburbs) where Muslim youth are concentrated was still a struggle. Blaming rap musicians for the outbreak of violence shifted focus away from the *political* causes of unrest, namely the government's policy of benign neglect.

More cynically, government agencies may use the social problems associated with youth and subcultures as a pretext for increased **surveillance** and **suppression**. For example, crime control and anti-terrorism measures may ultimately have marginal impacts on our safety but severe impacts on our freedom (Altheide 2006). In the "Chinese Columbine" example above, Communist Party officials used the fire, a tragic but isolated incident, to increasingly regulate and monitor internet usage, especially by young people, including restricting access to Western news (see

Jenkins 2002). Patricia and Peter Adler (2012) explain this process as a **control paradigm**, meaning

> a model of clear and present danger that can be expanded to implicate and oppress multitudes ... [where] a problem provides the pretext to regulate "undesirable" behavior. The objective has less to do with *personal safety* than with social control.

In most cases there is a "real" problem, as in the case of teen pregnancy and school shootings. However, instead of sex education or anti-bullying programs, too many schools rely upon largely symbolic fixes that satisfy certain political requirements without rocking the boat too much. In the case of school shootings, "weird" kids, "loners," and subcultural youth may become the focus of prevention efforts, even though the Secret Service published a study of 37 school shootings, reporting that: "There is no accurate or useful profile of students who engaged in targeted school violence." "Abstinence only" programs teach kids that the only way to avoid pregnancy and sexually transmitted infections is to avoid all sexual contact. Again, such solutions may satisfy political agendas, may even "work" for some youth, but are largely ineffective as social policy.

Politicians, police, religious leaders, and media figures can get away with these sorts of things because they typically have more legitimacy than subculturists – it's easy to believe the metalhead who wears a "satanic" shirt might be up to no good, *and* it's easy to believe the authority figures who accuse him of wrongdoing. Take the case of the West Memphis Three in which authorities accused three Arkansas youth of murdering three young boys. During their original trial, prosecutors claimed the three were part of a satanic cult, emphasizing their habit of wearing black clothing, their love of heavy metal music, and Damien Echols' expressed interest in Wicca and the occult. Such facts became fodder for **retrospective reinterpretation** – once a person has a stigmatizing label, we reinterpret past behaviors, beliefs, even appearance in light of the new label (Schur 1971). In the case of the West Memphis Three, once authorities arrested and accused the boys of murder, the media, the public, and likely even jurors reinterpreted their past interests and actions. *Of course* the three were guilty – they listened to heavy metal music, wore black clothing, and were "no good" kids. The case of Norwegian racist Anders Behring Breivik above is another perfect example. He perpetrates an horrific massacre and, seeking explanation, the media draws attention to his previous interests in gaming, implying games played a role in the killings.

KEY INSIGHTS

- Moral panics are recurring social phenomena that follow relatively (but not totally) predictable patterns and include reoccurring roles such as moral entrepreneurs, rule creators, and rule enforcers.
- As sociologist Barry Glassner suggests in his book *Culture of Fear*, we often fear the "wrong" things, that is, there are events and conditions that will likely do us more harm.
- Politicians or other authority figures often fuel, or even manufacture, such fears for political advantage or financial gain.
- While subculturists often garner significant negative attention, the larger society tends to gradually incorporate their values and practices into mainstream use, sometimes defusing subcultural values of their subversive intent.

EXPLORING FURTHER

Moral Panics: The Social Construction of Deviance (2nd edition), by Erich Goode and Nachman Ben-Yehuda, 2009 (Wiley-Blackwell). An updated version of a classic text, including discussions of terrorism, school shootings, and the "sex-slave" trade.

Critical Readings: Moral Panics and the Media, by Chas Critcher, 2003 (Open University Press). Compares the American and British perspectives on moral panics while examining AIDS, pedophilia, drugs, and other panics.

Moral Panics, by Kenneth Thompson, 1998 (Routledge). Another classic overview of the moral panic concept.

Folk Devils and Moral Panics, by Stanley Cohen, 2011 (Routledge). An updated version of the classic text on moral panics.

The Outsiders, directed by Francis Ford Coppola, 1983. A drama about a rivalry between the working class "greasers" and the more well-to-do "socs" that nicely illustrates assumptions made about youth from different social backgrounds, as illustrated by the Chambliss study in the chapter introduction.

Paradise Lost: The Child Murders at Robin Hood Hills (and sequels), directed by Joe Berlinger and Bruce Sinofsky, 1996. Filmed as the West Memphis Three went to trial, this stunning documentary demonstrates how a community's moral panic around satanism and heavy metal fueled the conviction of three social misfits who liked Metallica and black clothing. There are two sequels also worth watching.

West of Memphis, directed by Amy Berg, 2012. This documentary, again about the West Memphis Three, picks up the story of the three's 18-year fight to be released from prison. The film features more evidence of the men's innocence, revealing interviews with new witnesses, and an explanation of how police elicit false confessions.

Reefer Madness, directed by Louis J. Gasnier, 1936. Now a cult classic, this propaganda film depicts a group of young people whose drug use leads to rape, murder, and insanity. Meant to scare potential pot smokers straight, it has become a comedy to which some potheads get stoned.

7

HAVE SUBCULTURES GONE VIRTUAL? GLOBAL?

WHERE DO SUBCULTURISTS HANG OUT?

I have been extremely fortunate to visit several different countries and while abroad I enjoy seeking out subcultural spaces. While corporate globalization is easy to spot – McDonalds, Taco Bell, KFC – *subcultural* globalization is evident as well. As I browsed in a Brisbane record shop catering to punk and hardcore, I noticed the many similarities in fashions and even the musical styles between the US and Australia. I have discussed the merits of metal bands Black Sabbath and Iron Maiden in Costa Rica, and argued with a Costa Rican *Star Wars* fanatic over which film is the best. I saw Icelandic hardcore band I Adapt in a crowded Reykjavik café and gave some change to panhandling crust punks in Vancouver. In Peru, I was surprised by the popularity of the South Korean K-pop scene, while in Estonia I learned about Tallinn's underground raves. And at home in the US I've watched Japanese manga and anime subcultures gain increasing popularity. On top of that, straight edge kids from more than 20 countries such as the Philippines, Germany, Indonesia, and Brazil, have sent me emails since my book *Straight Edge* was published. Who could have predicted that over the course of 40 years or so that subcultures, even supposedly *underground* subcultures, would become so thoroughly global?

This chapter begins with a discussion of the environments in which subcultures exist, and how those environments, or "subcultural geographies," shape participants' experience. I discuss the importance of space and place as well as local, translocal, and virtual scenes before considering how the internet and digital media have transformed subcultures. The chapter then questions how subcultures spread around the world and ends by examining subculturists' embracement of and resistance to globalization.

SPACE AND PLACE: IN WHAT SORTS OF ENVIRONMENTS DO SUBCULTURES EXIST?

Like everyone else, subculturists exist in physical (and virtual) places, and such places impact the emergence and experience of subcultures. Where would skaters or traceurs be without the urban jungle providing them countless obstacles from which to perform their gravity-defying tricks? **Place** constitutes (1) geographic location, (2) material (and, I argue below, virtual) form, and, most especially, (3) the social meanings given to spaces, how we experience and interpret them (Gieryn 2000). Early scholars of subcultures and gangs were especially preoccupied with young people's (particularly working-class men's) occupation of the streets (Valentine et al. 1998). In contrast, **space** signifies abstract distances, volumes, geometries, and so on, absent social meaning. Spaces "set the stage for certain kinds of human activities" (Chen et al. 2013: 8). *Spaces* become *places* when occupied, used, and given meaning by people; places become spaces when "the unique gathering of things, meanings, and values are sucked out" (Gieryn 2000: 465). Put another way, "What begins as undifferentiated space becomes place as we get to know it better and endow it with value" (Tuan 2011 [1977]: 6). Passing by 315 Bowery at Bleecker Street in Manhattan one would notice a small shop front; however, knowing the space was the former site of the legendary CBGB music venue imbues the place with a special significance. Subculturists designate certain places as "cool" and others as boring or mundane (see Skelton and Valentine 1998). Thus during the week, as tourists disperse, blues clubs become nocturnal "havens" for musicians and regular patrons, offering a "vision of urban community and moral order" (Grazian 2003: 90). The club space helps manufacture a "brotherhood of strangers" in which people appreciate seeing familiar faces, even if they do not have close relationships.

The **emplacement** of subcultures, or their relationship to place, matters because subculturists often upend the meanings of and assumptions about spaces and places. In fact, particular spaces *make possible* certain subcultures. Take for example the bike messengers studied by Jeffrey Kidder (2011). Without the traffic gridlock in congested urban centers, messengers would not experience the danger, the thrill so central to their existence. Rather than seeing traffic as an irritation, messengers transform the "urban death maze" into a challenging playground in which their work – delivering packages – becomes play. The intense concentration and emotion messengers feel as they weave in and out of traffic (what Kidder calls the **affective appropriation of space**) offer moments of creativity and liberation in what can otherwise be stifling, exploitative environments. Likewise, subcultural identities are often intimately tied to space/place. For many hip hop cultures, "space is a dominant concern," as "the ghetto, 'hood, street, and corner all surface as representations of a particular image inscribing an ideal of authenticity or 'hardcore' urban reality" (Forman 2002: 3,5). Such urban spaces, real, imaginary, or somewhere in between, are more than simply settings in which subcultures "happen." Rather, places are "players" in social life, shaping, enabling, and constraining subculturists' activities and identities. (And places also become marketing tools, as promoters seek to capitalize on "real" Mississippi blues, or "genuine" Compton gangsta rap!)

Subculturists often come into conflict with authorities seeking to regulate subcultural places, such as enforcing curfews to keep youth off the streets. Police sought to reduce soccer hooliganism in the UK by eliminating standing terraces, by increasing security, and by installing closed-circuit security cameras across the grounds, pushing the clashes between firms even more into neighborhoods and train stations. Tired of the damage skaters inflict on benches and curbs, many cities have implemented skateboarding bans in certain areas, prompting skaters to post "skateboarding is not a crime" stickers. Likewise, while graffiti-writers see street art as changing bland spaces into beautiful places, shop-owners and municipal leaders often do not share their sentiments. As part of the ecstasy scares of the 1990s, authorities sought to regulate or eliminate underground raves, passing legislation threatening property owners who let their buildings be used for raves. Space is so central to subcultural experience that **spatial regulation** is one of the primary means of regulating subcultures more generally. Thus Chinese and Iranian authorities seek to regulate virtual spaces in an effort to forestall undesirable youth movements and other deviant groups.

Subculturists and others therefore contest the meaning and uses of space and place. Efforts to "clean up" public spaces and control "troublesome" youth limit the spaces in which subculturists can safely congregate. Spaces occupied by subculturists, including even streets and parks, serve as **free spaces** in which they can experiment with identities – as well as sex, drugs, and alcohol – relatively free from commercial interests and adult supervision (Robinson 2009). Subculturists might also fight over space, especially in local scenes, a classic (if wildly exaggerated) example being conflicts in the 1960s between mods and rockers in the UK. During the 1990s in the US, rap artists, promoters, and record labels played up an East Coast vs. West Coast rivalry, giving place sometimes deadly significance, while even jazz clubs become central to disputes about authenticity (Becker 2004).

LOCAL, TRANSLOCAL, AND VIRTUAL SCENES: HOW ARE SUBCULTURISTS CONNECTED?

Scholars often think about subcultures in terms of local, translocal, and virtual scenes (see Bennett and Peterson 2004). **Local scenes** form around specific geographical areas, incorporating and reflecting local issues, politics, and cultural practices and usually including face-to-face interaction (e.g. Shank 1994). Some subcultures maintain a very localized presence, never significantly spreading beyond their region of origin. Go-go music, a percussive blend of funk, R&B, and hip hop, emerged in Washington, DC's African American communities during the 1970s, responding to the racial strife and white flight that began in the previous decade (Hopkinson 2012). The scene supported a variety of black-owned businesses, including ticket sales, music clubs, and fashion boutiques, but never really made it out of DC. Likewise, the Sharpies – a 60s and 70s Australian subculture reminiscent of UK skinheads but with mullets and cardigan sweaters – was nearly exclusive to Melbourne. However, even seemingly grassroots, local scenes have ties to other distant scenes, and even parallel other contemporary local scenes; go-go borrows from Latin music as well as disco and hip hop. The Sharpie scene shared stylistic elements not just with mods and skinheads, but also glam and rock, even as they often sought to define themselves in opposition to such scenes (Bessant 1995).

Translocal scenes encompass various local scenes connected through shared subcultural values, styles, practices, and often music rather than frequent face-to-face contact (Kruse 1993). Translocal scenes exist regionally, nationally, or, as I discuss later, even globally. What connects such scenes, what holds them together? Music festivals, 'zines, consumer styles, and of course social media connect subculturists across sometimes vast distances. The Wacken Open Air metal festival in Germany brings together metal bands and fans from around Europe and even the world. In addition to these "concrete" connections, subculturists share more abstract identities and tastes (Kruse 1993; Hodkinson 2002). Thus despite their different experiences, Indonesian and North American punks would have much in common, sharing a very meaningful identity and likely listening to similar music.

Virtual scenes include the digital spaces in which subculturists interact, hang out, and ultimately form communities. Such **computer-mediated communities** may be diffuse and transient, but virtual scenes have a degree of consistency, some sense of norms, and include ongoing interaction and relationships. In other words, surfing steampunk websites does not automatically make one part of the steampunk scene (see Haenfler 2012c). The online *interactions*, the ongoing relationships, the emergent meanings, and the collective identification with steampunk constitute the virtual scene. Some subculturists have little, if any, connection to "face-to-face" or corporeal scenes. They interact *primarily* via the internet; in other words, virtual scenes are more than additional spaces through which local scenes interact. The web can play an enormous role in creating or coalescing a scene, as in the alternative country (or "alt. country") scene, bringing together musicians and fans of country music "mixed with attitude" (Lee and Peterson 2004: 188).

While dividing scenes into such "layers" makes intuitive sense, a local scene is not a "closed system of social relations but a particular articulation of contacts and influences drawn from a variety of places scattered, according to power-relations, fashion and habit, across many different parts of the globe" (Massey 1998: 124). Subcultures (and cultures more broadly) are products of interaction, and people consistently interact across these layers. A local burlesque community has translocal and virtual influences and contacts. Further, a local scene in a major metropolitan area may be "bigger" (i.e. including more people and covering greater geographic space) than a small national or regional scene.

SUBCULTURES ONLINE: HOW HAVE SCENES CHANGED WITH NEW MEDIA?

With the advent of new media, in particular the constant access to digital entertainment, communication, and community via the internet, subcultural places exist increasingly online. Facebook, Twitter, Instagram, MySpace, YouTube, Pandora, Spotify, Pinterest, Tumblr, and other **social media** offer subculturists new ways to connect and by the time you read this book, new social media platforms will likely exist. Imagine how being punk has changed from 1977 to 2013. In the 70s, seeing an underground punk band play required attending a show; to buy their music you had to locate a specialty shop; reading about them meant acquiring a print fanzine; and to share your interest with others, you had to discover local punk hangouts or even – gasp – *write a letter*! Today, YouTube provides access to dozens of live performances; you can digitally download the band's music from their website, iTunes, or even illegally; online 'zines make reading interviews easy; and digital forums fill with fans arguing the merits of the band's latest record. The internet makes it easier for people around the world to discover, enjoy, share, and contribute to subcultural products. Social media can even empower people to circumvent government restrictions. (Although it also offers authorities new means of surveillance.) Some countries prevented the sale of punk, metal, even many kinds of Western pop music – for young Iranians, the internet was *the only* way to listen to metal.

Thus the conventional notion of subcultures as local scenes embedded in physical space and characterized by face-to-face interaction is at least partially obsolete (Bennett and Robards 2012). Yet it may be tempting to think of virtual scenes or virtual participation as less "real" than interactions in physical spaces; if "places" require material form, online interaction is artificial. For example, some people scoff at the notion of online dating sites or relationship-seeking chatrooms, suggesting that drunken conversation in a pub is somehow more "real." However, while virtual and non-virtual communities differ in some significant ways, they share remarkable similarities, suggesting no compelling reason to judge one arena less authentic (although subculturists may do so!). The terms "virtual" and "real" reinforce the idea that digital spaces are less authentic, meaningful, and significant than non-virtual spaces. Yet virtual scenes *are* real, in that they involve real people experiencing subjectively "genuine" interaction. Better to ask how virtual scenes *differ from* and (often) *coincide with* non-virtual scenes.

With feet firmly planted in both virtual and non-virtual settings, subculturists demonstrate that the real/virtual *dichotomy* is really a *dialectic*, producing something new from the intersection of the two. Traceurs often initially encountered parkour online, inspired to begin their own training by practitioners sometimes half a world away (Kidder 2012). They then attempt to replicate tricks and moves performed in a far off city or country in their own local, corporeal settings. Eventually, some will film and post their own exploits online, all the while discussing and sharing stories and ideas with other traceurs. Thus the virtual is emplaced in the "real": "these real, physical practices are instantiations of far-off, ephemeral worlds lived on-screen" (Kidder 2012: 247–248).

ONLINE COMMUNITIES: OPPORTUNITIES OR CONSTRAINTS?

Issues of space are not confined to scenes located primarily in the physical realm. Digital architectures profoundly shape participants' experience in virtual scenes. Digital spaces create possibilities and constraints, much like offline settings. For example, stigmatized people connect with others sharing their experiences and interests. In Italy, emo kids use social networking sites to develop friendships and find acceptance amongst likeminded peers; "It was not the Web, as media panics would claim, that caused their isolation but the off-line context" (Seganti and Smahel 2011). Underground artists have greater opportunity to share their art and network with others. Graffiti-writers around the world use YouTube as a space "in which they can engage in, and support, creativity through social networking" by watching "how to" clips and sharing techniques via comments beneath the videos (Light et al. 2012: 344). Graffiti-writers' use of YouTube, much like the traceurs I mentioned above, also demonstrates how virtual and face-to-face interaction often overlap. Subculturists make plans to see a show on Twitter, post pictures and video of the show with Instagram and YouTube, talk about the show on Facebook, and listen to the bands on Spotify. Even participants in the largely virtual alt.country scene have organized face-to-face gatherings (Lee and Peterson 2004).

Yet for all their potential freedom, virtual scenes come with constraints. The anonymity of online forums, such as message boards and YouTube comments, promote flaming (making derisive comments) and trolling (being deliberately provocative), potentially policing creativity and boosting a scene's exclusivity. Timothy Rowlands' (2012) study of the fantasy massively multiplayer online game *Everquest* showed how the game design favored a particularly repetitive style of play in which players adopt a role (tank, healer, or damage dealer) and repeatedly kill monsters in a perpetual series of mouse clicks. The structure of the game worked against other, less instrumental, styles of play. Additionally, the accessibility of online subcultural communities makes them prime targets for sur-veillance and control. Already excellent targets for moral entrepre-neurial campaigns (see Chapter 6), virtual subcultures stoke worries about internet addiction, child predators, online gambling, and "subversive" activities.

Finally, it may be that virtual life, our "life on the screen," leaves us strangely, as Sherry Turkle puts it, "alone together" (Turkle 1995, 2011). Despite living in "real" spaces, we increasingly seek virtual escapes, leaving relationships more shallow and people simultaneously isolated even as they are connected. However, as traceurs, graffiti-writers, skaters, and other subculturists show, vir-tual spaces offer new ways with which to engage in physical spaces and experiences. "Real" life may be enhanced by technology and social media rather than degraded (Kidder 2012).

VIRTUAL AUTHENTICITY AND IDENTITIES

I once interviewed a hardcore kid who lamented the decline of DIY distros and record shops. For him, eBay and other online auction sites made finding rare records too easy. Certainly he felt nostalgia for the days of flipping through record bins and making surprising discoveries, but his greater worry was that people who "didn't get it," who didn't *authentically* understand "his" music and scene, would be able to buy their way into the hardcore culture. Having the right subcultural networks and the commitment to acquire exclusive subcultural goods distinguished him from poseurs and wannabes. The explosive growth of virtual life requires rethinking many of the aspects of subcultures I have previously discussed. For example, how do subculturists measure authenticity when much of subcultural experience now takes place online? Studying online straight edge forums, Williams and Copes (2005) found that some straight edgers tied authenticity directly to participation in a (physical) hardcore scene; you couldn't *really* be straight edge if you only interacted with other straight edgers online. Others, however, contended that *online* participation, separate from the fashion show and scene politics of the hardcore scene, was more authentic. Thus virtual scenes provide fertile subject matter for discussions of authenticity – and the forums in which to have them!

Virtual communities also allow participants to experiment with identities not necessarily reflective of their corporeal bodies and offline presentation of self. A male gamer might enact a gender-bending performance while playing a female avatar in an online game, and an otherwise "vanilla" suburban mom can post her erotic *Twilight* stories on fan fiction sites. Like anyone, subculturists might worry that people misrepresent themselves online. Yet many virtual spaces facilitate radical *honesty* rather than deception, with people sharing intimate details of their lives (Bortree 2005). The main point is that virtual scenes offer subculturists expanded, but not unlimited, opportunities to play with identities.

WILL VIRTUAL WORLDS SET US FREE?

Utopian visions of virtual spaces suggest new opportunities to experiment with identities, freeing people, in a sense, from their corporeal limitations and even their social class, lineage, age, race, and gender. Online gaming, for example, commonly enables players to choose their avatar's gender, race, and profession, and success seemingly depends upon the time and commitment one invests rather than ascribed privileges such as family wealth. Anyone can be a hero. Yet gaming cultures largely reproduce the same social exclusion present in the non-virtual world (Embrick et al. 2012). Virtual games often glorify hypermasculine behavior, depict racial minorities in one-dimensional ways, and reinforce heterocentrism. And while gaming advertisements depict women and racial minorities in numbers approximating their proportion of the US population, the adverts sexualize women and limit black men to stereotypical roles of athletes, thugs, or military personnel (Peck et al. 2011).

SUBCULTURES AND GLOBALIZATION: HOW DO SUBCULTURES TRAVEL?

Despite my travels and the friendships I've made abroad, I am still at times startled to learn just how global subcultures have become: *How did a punk scene blossom in China? Who brought hip hop to Egypt? How did manga take off in the US? There is a doom metal scene in Japan!?* Even relatively small, underground subcultures find diverse adherents in a rapidly globalizing world.

In a basic sense, **globalization** involves the ongoing process of economic, political, and cultural integration (Eckes and Zeiler 2003). Economically, local and global markets increasingly merge as both capital and goods move around the world. Politically, nations' fates become ever more intertwined, with organizations such as the International Monetary Fund, the United Nations, the European Union, and the World Bank making attempts at transnational or global governance. And culturally, diverse peoples share art, music, food, film, literature, and fashion in unprecedented ways. Digital technology, global mass media, and air travel make the world seem smaller, at least to those with access, even changing our sense of time and space (Giddens 1991a). But what does globalization mean for *subcultures*?

To start, globalization fosters transnational subcultural economies, as participants create and trade their goods (e.g. music, skateboarding films, 'zines) across the world. Politically, globalization enables subcultures to share often deviant or even subversive ideologies. And culturally, globalization facilitates the rapid sharing of musical innovations, dance styles, and fashion sensibilities. But just how does this happen, and what are globalization's effects?

CULTURAL SHARING/NETWORKING: HOW DO SUBCULTURES SPREAD?

It is relatively easy to see how Hollywood films make their way to nearly every corner of the earth. Multinational corporations with vested commercial interests use their resources to produce and market movies with broad appeal, even creating films heavy on action and light on dialogue to be more palatable to non-native English speakers. Subcultures typically spread via somewhat less strategic or instrumental means. By definition, subcultures do not enjoy mass appeal and cannot mobilize an army of marketers and other professionals. In fact, sometimes subculturists oppose increased visibility, wary that their scene might get "too big," thereby escaping their control and undermining their authenticity. (Of course that doesn't prevent entrepreneurs, both corporate and subcultural, from appropriating and selling subcultures, as we saw in Chapter 5.)

Cultural diffusion involves the spread of all sorts of cultural artifacts between individuals and groups. **Centralized diffusion** occurs when governments or corporations actively promote or even impose an idea or product on less powerful groups or societies. MTV has expanded around the globe – MTV Europe, MTV Japan, MTV Latin America, MTV Arabia, and so on, guided by elites with particular viewpoints and agendas. Somewhat similarly, subcultures spread as the result of subcultural entrepreneurs such as record label owners, but usually on a much smaller scale. **Decentralized diffusion** is less planned, less controlled, and less characterized by power imbalances. Examples include heavy metal fans trading tapes internationally, underground punk bands setting up DIY shows abroad, riot grrrls sending 'zines to other countries, and, of course, the many subcultural exchanges via the internet. Consider the tattoo and body modification subcultures. Tattooing originated in many ancient cultures and the international tattoo scene emerged from a variety of decentralized exchanges as artists and tattooees travelled abroad, building social ties from the ground up. Now, however, the mass-marketing of tattoo culture via reality TV shows and tattoo-inspired apparel may introduce more centralized diffusion. Subcultures spread via both centralized and decentralized processes, though if we think of diffusion as a continuum between the two, subcultural diffusion *tends* to be less centralized than pop culture explicitly mass-marketed for broad global appeal.

Immigrants often facilitate subcultural globalization, much as West Indian workers shared elements of their cultures with working-class Britons. When people move, voluntarily or involuntarily, en masse to new homelands the resulting **diaspora** communities often maintain real and symbolic connections with their "motherland." Chinese American rapper Jin found modest success in the US but greater acclaim in Hong Kong. Similarly, Japanese American emcee Ai found huge success in Japan. Such bilingual artists facilitate subcultural exchange in both directions.

RIOT GRRRL GOES INTERNATIONAL

Determined to make their own, feminist-inspired media since the early 1990s, riot grrrls have long championed women as cultural producers rather than passive consumers. In addition to 'zine making, riot grrrl inspired Ladyfests, "DIY festivals organized by women to showcase female talents, speak out against sexism, racism, and homophobia, and to encourage women and girls to become active creators of their own culture, entertainment, and politics" (Schilt and Zobl 2008: 177). In the 2000s, the internet helped renew interest in DIY feminist punk politics around the world – Kristen Schilt and Elke Zobl (2008) found 'zine editors and Ladyfests in 30 countries. These 'zines and fests have produced an international network of feminist girls and women, as well as transgender and queer youth.

As nations democratize, become economically integrated, and gain access to digital media and communications, they become more open to subcultural diffusion (Mayer 2011). There is little doubt that the digital revolution I discussed above played an enormous role in the diffusion of subcultural ideas since the early 1990s. Adam Mayer (2011) used an internet archive to measure the number of heavy metal bands in 150 countries from 1991–2007. Despite the music's marginal commercial viability and little cultural acceptability, metal spread fastest to countries with greatest **digital capacity**, that is most access to personal computing and the internet. Metalheads around the world had long traded cassette tapes, forming an underground network of fans. This underground network expanded exponentially with the ease of internet communication. Importantly, the diffusion of metal was less the result of some hegemonic corporate push into new markets as it was a decentralized, more grassroots effort by metalheads.

HOMOGENIZATION OR HYBRIDITY: DOES GLOBALIZATION *DESTROY* LOCAL SUBCULTURES?

As local spaces and places seemingly give way to global and virtual scenes, perhaps elites have even greater control over cultural production, appropriating and/or infiltrating local cultures to satisfy the whims of the market. Colonialism and economic and political domination have allowed the US, UK, and continental Europe to disproportionately influence cultural production in the rest of the world, exerting a **cultural hegemony** outstripping what one might expect given their populations. Put bluntly, do subcultures around the world simply imitate their North American and European counterparts?

The short answer is no. Despite the global economy and media, we are a long way off from an international monoculture. In fact, globalization has in some ways **fragmented** societies, dividing us into ever more narrow "tribes" based upon religion, politics, ethnicity, and subcultural interests (Touraine 2000). Rather than passively absorbing and mimicking cultural imports, local subculturists adopt and adapt (sub)cultural imports according to their own, indigenous interests (Craig 2003). Japan's Visual Kei – a music and fashion scene combining goth, metal, and glam rock – infuses metal with kabuki-like theatricality. Japanese emcees combine samurai imagery with American gangsta motifs (Condry 2006). What's more, subculturists in Asia and the Global South self-consciously address the influence of the US, as I discuss below.

Roland Robertson (1995) claims that the global and local continually *interact* or in fact are not separate at all but rather interdependent. **Glocalization**, the process by which local people use, adopt, adapt, and reject translocal culture, suggests that while people in local contexts certainly feel the influence of global pressures, they filter those influences through their local experience, needs, and opportunities. The global is more local than we might think, and vice versa. For example, do local radio stations play international music? Do local radio stations even *exist* in some parts of the world? Such questions reveal the relationship between the local and global. Observing women in Mexico's Yucatan making tortillas in the traditional Mayan way alongside youth playing video games in an internet café, Doreen Massey (1998: 122) notes the coexistence of local traditions and global influences. Subcultures, then, are neither "closed" local cultures nor "undifferentiatedly global." They are not tied to geographic space, but they exist within local geographies.

While young Burmese emcees appreciate Western rap, hip hop in Burma is relatively tame by US standards, focusing more on romance and unrequited love than misogynist boasting and sexually explicit lyrics (Keeler 2009). This is due in part to government censorship of more controversial topics and in part to the country's Buddhist traditions and a sense that sexually provocative lyrics would shame one's family. Burmese rappers adopt the bass–driven sonic styles and performative demeanors of US hip hop, but avoid the ultraviolence of gangsta rap as well as the politics of conscious rap. The display of power that rap affords appeals to young men in both Burma and the US (and elsewhere), but how emcees ultimately perform rap depends upon local contexts (Keeler 2009). Mass communications and digital technologies may have accelerated the creation of "global teens," cosmopolitan, mostly middle-class young people who share many interests, practices, and cultural sensibilities, but they appropriate subcultural themes to their own ends (see Acland 2000).

Subcultures seem to exemplify cultural **hybridity**, in which translocal beliefs and practices are mutually influential, rather than determined by a hegemonic power. So punks in China, France, and Argentina may be distinct, but they often share common symbols and influences, influences drawn from, but not exclusive to, the West. Likewise, metalheads in Brazil, Iraq, and Canada share their outsider status, not to mention their love of metal music, dark clothing, and macabre imagery. Yet local concerns and national politics shape subcultural expression in each of these countries, making them far more than clones of the global metal scene. In the small African nation of Botswana, a subculture of metalheads has grown since its inception in the early 1990s (Banchs 2013). Some bands, such as Wrust, focus on universal metal themes such as alienation, while others such as Skinflint incorporate African mythology into their lyrics. Some Batswana metalheads dress in the black t-shirts common around the world, while others adopt retro head-to-toe leather outfits – complete with studs and cowboy hats – regardless of the desert heat (Barnett 2012).

Still, despite growing access to digital technology, subcultural exchanges do not flow equally between all parts of the world. Cultural diffusion is not an equal process, an egalitarian give and take between nations or groups of equal power. Alan O'Connor's work reveals important differences in punk based in Toronto, Mexico City, Washington, DC, and Barcelona, differences corresponding to differences in social structure. These punks have varying access to venues, touring bands, and radio stations. North American bands, with greater resources to record and tour, are more likely to influence Mexican punk than vice versa (O'Connor 2002, 2004). Language proves another barrier to equal exchange, as US subculturists are less open to music sung in languages other than English and, given the plethora of English-language music in their preferred genres, have less need to branch out. Therefore the **global center** (or core nations) *does* disproportionately influence subcultural production when compared to so-called **periphery** nations. At the time the only metal festival in the Middle East, the Dubai Desert Rock Fest was dominated by international acts from the US, UK, and Sweden. That does not, of course, preclude Middle Eastern bands from putting their own stamp on metal. But European and North American metal subcultures exert a powerful influence. What's more, periphery countries play another role in subcultural production as they manufacture subcultural products for consumption elsewhere. Most metal (and punk, etc.) shirts are made in countries such as China, places where relatively few major bands have ever played.

MODS AROUND THE WORLD

The mods originated primarily among working-class youth in 1960s UK. In contrast to their leather-clad, motorcycle-riding rocker counterparts, the mods' dapper clothes and stylish scooters symbolized a focus on idealism, progress, and the future. Christine Feldman (2009) shows how, even prior to Tumblr and YouTube, mod culture spread around the world, including to Germany and Japan. Youth in these and other countries, already influenced by jazz and rock 'n' roll, encountered mod via the music of the Beatles and The Who and, earlier, American and British GIs who occupied each country for a time. While mods everywhere share fashions, music, and a focus on the "modern," mod emerged in each country to fill different needs. For German youth, mod was an opportunity to "react against the Nazi past and to think globally verses nationalistically" (Feldman 2009: 65). Mod came to Japan in the wake of the continued recovery from the destruction of World War II, in which the future took the form of devastating nuclear bombs. As the Japanese rebuilt their cities and psyches, mods helped create a more hopeful vision of the future. Today, Japanese mods may be the "most mod" of all, both in outlook and in their steadfast display of mod subcultural styles.

RESISTANCE AND GLOBALIZATION

Far from creating universal justice and democracy, globalization has simply redistributed wealth and privilege in new ways. As Zygmunt Bauman suggests: "Glocalization is first and foremost a redistribution of privileges and deprivations, of wealth and poverty, of resources and impotence, of power and powerlessness, of freedom and constraint. It is, one may say, a process of world-wide *restratification*" (in Beilharz 2000: 304). Many so-called "developing" countries remain in staggering debt to international banks, a result of colonialism and dictators' mismanagement (and theft). In exchange for loans, organizations such as the International Monetary Fund and the World Bank force these "heavily-indebted nations" to accept economic reforms (often called "structural adjustment programs") that generally privatize formerly public goods and services (e.g. water). Critics argue that elites (e.g. heads of international organizations, government officials/dictators, and bankers) make such arrangements to the detriment of the vast majority of citizens, undermining democracy and reinforcing poverty (Bauman 1998, 2011; Stiglitz 2003). While many youth embrace global cosmopolitanism, subcultures have at times marshaled resistance to globalization. Some bands for whom English is not their first language still sing in English in order to broaden their appeal. Others, however, purposefully sing in their native tongue even while capable of singing in English to defy cultural hegemony and to boost their local or national authenticity. Punks in Mexico have joined anti-globalization activists, holding benefits for the Zapatista movement and protesting alongside university students (O'Connor 2003b) while hip hop continues to serve as a medium of opposition. Mwenda Ntarangwi (2009: 3) argues that East African youth use hip hop to voice opposition to and raise awareness against the negative effects of globalization and to raise awareness about HIV/AIDS. Yet without globalization, these youth would have never encountered hip hop. And just as hip hop becomes a means of voicing dissent, it simultaneously provides a small income, offering opportunities along with setbacks.

Subculturists also use cultural imports to signal their **resistance to their natal culture** and as a means of distinction, a way to "be cool," by using such imports as subcultural capital. For example, the metal scene in India has only recently grown significantly. Some Indian metalheads see metal as a way to resist the Bollywood music/film industry, as one fan explains: "For [Indian metalheads], metal is a way to connect to a global culture and break free from the restrictions they feel in their traditional society" (Dunn and McFadyen 2008). Brazilian speed metal band Sepultura challenged the notion of "national music" by adopting an international genre far different from the *música popular brasileira* centered around acoustic singer/songwriters and considered sophisticated by the middle class (Avelar 2011). Eventually, the band embraced afro-Brazilian percussion and also recorded with the indigenous Xavante tribe, questioning conventional understandings of "Brazilian" music and consequently Brazilian identity. Similarly, Indonesian youths' adoption of international music provides some national connections amidst religious, ethnic, and class divisions that pose a threat to national unity in the post-Suharto era (Wallach 2008).

To some, globalization represents a threat to national interests and identity, the desire for subcultural music, styles, and ideas representing a danger to dominant traditions and social hierarchies.

While political and religious leaders may condemn pop culture in general, subcultural diffusion gains significant attention, perhaps because spectacular scenes are easily stigmatized and, often populated by young people with relatively few resources, easier to repress. In socialist Europe, the Communist Party sought to quash subcultural expression, its agenda one of minimizing deviance and difference and maximizing patriotism and collectivism (Pilkington 1994). Worried that outside (sub)cultural influences would undermine the socialist ideology, the Communist Party sought to defend itself against Western influence, treating "deviant" youth as victims of propaganda (Pilkington and Omel'chenko 2013). They had cause for alarm. Prior to the fall of communism, underground musicians in Hungary based much of their subcultural identity around opposition to the state socialist government (Szemere 2001).

Similarly, various Islamic governments have feared the influence of Western values and lifestyles. Fearing music's political influence, several Middle Eastern countries outlawed rap, metal, and reggae, which only served to push the scenes underground (Levine 2008). Metal CDs and t-shirts were forbidden in Iran (Dunn and McFadyen 2008). Those advocating traditional, conservative Islamic agendas may have reason to worry. Just as European and North American black metal musicians skewered Christianity, Middle Eastern bands are using the genre to blast Islam (Kelly 2012). Motivated by the murder of her parents by a suicide bomber, Iraqi group Janaza's *female* singer screams "Burn the Quran! Burn the fucking Quran!"

IS GLOBALIZATION REALLY SO NEW?

While the effect of social media and digital participation on subcultures is profound, one could easily *overstate* their impact. Even prior to the digital revolution the notion of self-contained, local scenes may have been exaggerated. While it might seem like the globalization of subcultures rests upon the internet, subcultures have *always* been mediated, have always had channels through which to spread. Deep Purple and Kiss were playing Japan long before the web, building the foundation for a hard rock and metal scene that continues today. Russian youth encountered Western rock 'n' roll via short-wave radio, tape recorders, and Soviet sailors who had traveled abroad, despite the government prohibiting such music (Yurchak 1999). Mod, punk, body modification, and burlesque all traveled internationally prior to the internet. Thus while globalization has become an academic and journalistic buzzword, many of the changes we associate with contemporary digital globalization have deep roots. Hip hop brought together African American, African, and Caribbean influences well before the digital revolution.

The internet may have accelerated the spread and blending of scenes, but subcultures drew from many sources long before going online. Subculturists and subcultural historians often try to capture the "authentic" history of localized scenes, yet such histories often leave out significant parts of the story. Mod, one of the quintessential working class British postwar subcultures, drew influence from American modern jazz, R&B, and advertising; Jewish, gay, and Caribbean club scenes; and French, Italian, and Scandinavian fashions and designs (Feldman 2009). Likewise the argument over whether punk emerged in the US or the UK leaves out the significant exchanges between the two countries that resulted in what became punk (Haenfler, forthcoming).

KEY INSIGHTS

- Space and place create, limit, and shape the possibilities for subcultural expression; *where* subculturists hang out influences how they participate, who takes part, and how they construct authenticity.
- Authorities often regulate subcultural spaces as part of general efforts to monitor and control deviant groups.
- The internet, social media, and expanding global markets have accelerated the spread of subcultures around the world. However, translocal, even global scenes existed *prior* to the digital revolution.
- While participants in translocal subcultures have much in common, locals adapt subcultural styles, values, identities, and practices to their own surroundings, their own needs.
- While subculturists typically embrace (and even take advantage of) the globalization of scenes, they also use subcultural resources to *resist* what they see as the more egregious effects of globalization.

EXPLORING FURTHER

Music Scenes: Local, Translocal, and Virtual, edited by Andy Bennett and Richard A. Peterson, 2004 (Vanderbilt University Press). A collection of studies from blues and karaoke to anarchopunk and alt.country, divided into local, translocal, and virtual scenes.

The Hood Comes First: Race, Space, and Place in Rap and Hip Hop, by Murray Forman, 2002 (Wesleyan University Press). A critical look at how inner-city spaces and places shape racial constructions, representations, and resistance in hip hop.

Cool Places: Geographies of Youth Cultures, edited by Tracey Skelton and Gill Valentine, 1998 (Routledge). An interdisciplinary collection of papers exploring subcultural representations and resistances as well as subculturists in their homes, workplaces, and public spaces.

Hip Hop Japan: Rap and the Paths of Cultural Globalization, by Ian Condry, 2006 (Duke University Press). An ethnographic study of Japanese hip hop addressing how global influences are filtered through local spaces such as music clubs and record labels.

Metal Rules the Globe: Heavy Metal Music Around the World, edited by Jeremy Wallach, Harris M. Berger, and Paul D. Greene (Duke University Press). A collection of essays about metal in an amazing number of scenes across North and South America, Europe, and throughout Asia.

Hip Hop Africa: New African Music in a Globalizing World, edited by Eric Charry, 2012 (Wesleyan University Press). An engaging portrait of how African rappers across the continent blend global styles with local traditions.

Social Exclusion, Power and Video Game Play: New Research in Digital Media and Technology, edited by David G. Embrick, Talmadge J. Wright, and Andras Lukacs, 2012 (Lexington Books). Explores the limited capacity of online worlds to free us from the constraints, prejudices, and inequalities of the corporeal world.

Otaku Spaces and *The Otaku Encyclopedia: An Insider's Guide to the Subculture of Cool Japan*, by Patrick W. Galbraith, 2012 and 2009 (Chin Music Press and Kodansha USA). The first book includes photos by Androniki Christodoulou of Otaku homes, showing the connections between subculture and fandom. The second offers an introduction to otaku culture.

I ♥ Hip Hop in Morocco, directed by Joshua Asen and Jennifer Needleman, 2007. Documentary following young Moroccan hip hoppers as they attempt to stage a show despite resistance from more conservative elements of their society.

Bomb It, directed by John Reiss, 2007. A documentary following the exploits of graffiti artists on five continents.

Global Metal: 7 Countries, 3 Continents, 1 Tribe, directed by Sam Dunn and Scot McFadyen, 2008. Documentary exploring the worldwide community of heavy metal fans, from black metal in China to thrash in Iran.

Punk In Africa: Three Chords, Three Countries, One Revolution, directed by Keith Jones and Deon Maas, 2011. Documentary chronicling the history and politics of punk in South Africa, Mozambique, and Zimbabwe. www.punkinafrica.co.za.

8

WHAT HAPPENS TO SUBCULTURISTS AS THEY "GROW UP"?

In 2010, comedian and punk Jón Gnarr successfully led his Best Party to victory in the Reykjavik mayoral race (Birrell 2011). A self-described anarchist inspired by Gandhi and anarchopunk legends Crass, Gnarr and a cabinet full of former punks set out to transform politics, first by satirizing the entire process – they promised kids they would build a Disneyland and bring a polar bear to the zoo – and then by actually enacting policies – pushing forward with plans to make the city a hub for electric cars (McGrane 2010). A cadre of bankers and politicians had led Iceland into financial collapse in 2008, prompting disaffected voters to disrupt the status quo. Gnarr, who maintains he still wants to tear the system down, felt like he had to infiltrate politics to make real change. Subculturists are often cast as nihilistic kids with no future, exemplified by the Circle Jerks song "Live Fast Die Young." However, Gnarr's journey from sniffing glue and playing in punk band Nefrennsli ("Runny Nose") to Reykjavik city hall shows that subculturists may wind up in the most unlikely places. Their paths towards adulthood are rarely straightforward and many subculturists creatively find ways to live subcultural lives.

To be sure, many subculturists do "grow up," leaving behind their subcultural identities as they transition to work, career, and family. However, new research shows that subcultural participation resonates long into many adults' lives (Bennett 2013). Adults actually make up a *majority* in many subcultures. The tramp, or "hobo," subculture of late nineteenth and early twentieth century US consisted of single, homeless migrant working men who rode trains from town to town as they sought work harvesting crops (Harper 2006). Likewise, given the expense of customizing hot rod cars, Kustom Kulture draws a multigenerational, generally older, crowd. Often located amid urban nightlife, burlesque subcultures attract adult participants and audiences. In this chapter, I ask how subculturists transition from youth scenes to adulthood, how they transform subcultural styles and meanings, and how younger and older subculturists get along. I then explore how older subculturists reconcile their deviant identities with work, parenthood, and other "adult" responsibilities.

ARE SUBCULTURES JUST FOR KIDS?

As I have said, both the popular media and many researchers identify subcultures primarily with youth. One reason for this is that in the Chicago School era many scholars and social reformers studied immigrant or ethnic youth "gangs" with the intent of solving urban social problems. Groups of deviant young people became synonymous with crime and other social problems that capture public attention, sometimes escalating into moral panics. Still, until the middle of the twentieth century, kids grew up fairly fast, taking on "adult" responsibilities (such as farm work) relatively quickly. The whole notion of "youth" emerged as a distinctive life phase in the post-World War II era, as more young people had access to popular culture, higher education, and increasing disposable income, and as marketers sought to create a new marketing niche. Labor laws, rising standards of living, an expanding education system and other structural changes created more space for kids to be kids. Another explanation for the links between youth and subcultures is that youth in many cases are more likely to adopt the *spectacular* aspects of subcultures, the strange clothes and outlandish behavior that make subculturists stand out. Young subculturists might simply be more noticeable.

Of course subcultural identification and participation are not confined to youth. In fact, as young people put off the traditional markers of adulthood – careers, home ownership, marriage, children – it is unsurprising they might continue their subcultural pursuits. Young adulthood – perhaps better called *emerging* adulthood – can extend into one's late twenties and beyond. A variety of social forces have led to the continued expansion of "youthful" lifestyles: increased longevity may have youth thinking "what's the rush?" to grow up; greater competition for jobs prompts many to seek further education, extended the space between childhood and adulthood; and stagnating wages make buying a home and starting a family a daunting prospect. Still, many subculturists who *have* transitioned to adult roles and responsibilities maintain connections to scenes traditionally thought of as youth-oriented. And some people come to subcultures as adults rather than as youth.

NEW MEANINGS – LESS STYLE, MORE SUBSTANCE

Given the (both popular and scholarly) focus on subcultural style, it comes as little surprise that older subculturists, less prone to wearing bondage gear or molding their hair into impossible shapes, are often invisible. Just because many subculturists eventually mute their "spectacular" styles and become less involved does not mean they abandon their subcultural identities. Such identities become less of "tribal" affiliations and more personal philosophies, less about style and more about lifestyle or "internalized code" (Haenfler 2012a: 13; Bennett 2006). Dennis Lyxzén of Swedish straight edge hardcore band Refused explained that he rarely "advertised" his edge identity (such as by wearing Xs) but that straight edge still held an important place in his politics:

> I mean, it's one of those things where you feel that when you're young – or younger? Okay, let's say young – you have maybe a stronger need to define what you are and what you are against. In that sense straight edge was probably a good way to get into politics. But as far as the whole straight edge scene goes, I'm not involved in that today. It seems more like a youth cultural kind of thing, and I don't really feel any connection to it anymore. So, I don't X up, I don't call myself straight edge – but I'm still drug-free, and that's still a part of me I'm very comfortable with.
>
> (Kuhn 2010: 61)

For some, outward expressions of style gives way to a focus on personally meaningful subcultural values and practices, a transition Andes (1998) calls **transcendence**. Older straight edgers, for example, developed **strategies of style**, recognizing both its limits and potential (Haenfler 2012a). Style (such as X-ing up) was limiting when used to "prove" one's authenticity, when it interfered with work responsibilities, when it symbolized a narrow (often hypermasculine) music-based identity, and when it drew attention away from related issues such as vegetarianism. On the other hand, older straight edgers used style to connect with similarly-aged peers, as a way to keep the movement's legacy alive for younger adherents, and an as an overt symbol of resistance in their "adult" contexts. Strategically deploying Xs, tattoos, band t-shirts, or hoodies with straight edge slogans at work or certain social gatherings became ways of distancing oneself from the perceived undesirable attributes of adulthood, especially conformity. Of course focusing less on style than substance is also a way for older participants to position their authenticity (see Chapter 5).

Beyond style and beyond personal philosophy, some older subculturists increase their focus on subculturally-informed *politics*, putting their subcultural values into practice in new contexts. Women with roots in riot grrrl have formed Girls' Rock Camps, teaching girls to play music, create bands, make 'zines, and stage shows (Schilt and Giffort 2012). Such camps provide older riot grrrls with "an institutional location in which to share punk feminist ideologies, women's musical history and technical knowledge intergenerationally" (Schilt and Giffort 2012: 147). Keeping with DIY feminist riot grrrl politics, such camps offer "more than music," seeking to build self-esteem, foster community, and encourage cultural resistance to women's subordination. Organizers feel "they are complicating the idea of what it means to grow up and 'get a real job'" as well as the "assumption that marriage and children are the inevitable and only pathway for women" (Schilt and Giffort 2012: 154). Even rave, a scene often characterized as apolitical and hedonistic, can produce profound personal and political consequences for participants. Ex-raver women reported the scene boosted their confidence, helped them cultivate non-judgmental attitudes, *and* guided them into helping professions such as counseling (Gregory 2012).

AGEING BODIES

Ageing seems like a natural, inevitable, and often undesirable process: skin sags, wrinkles appear, muscles weaken, hair grays or disappears. Yet we interpret the *physical* signs of ageing through our cultural lenses. The physical signs of ageing take on social meanings, prescribing certain expectations regardless of our physical capabilities. For example, in many cultures an ageing double standard persists, in which men's ageing bodies grow more "distinguished" while women's ageing bodies are less valued. Modern medicine and better nutrition have steadily increased many people's average lifespan and allowed those with access the possibility of transcending physical limitations that might have been debilitating in generations past. Still, even as the meanings of ageing change, ageing bodies suggest certain social expectations captured by the admonition "Act your age!" Thus a 60ish-year-old body should not be moshing with 17-year-olds! The physicality of moshing – whether the average 60-year-old body can withstand the bumps and bruises of the pit – is significant, but in some ways beside the point. Moshing seems, to many observers, somehow *inappropriate*, even *unbecoming*, for people of a certain age.

Fonorow (1997) found that where someone positions their body at an indie music gig symbolized their connection with the band and the scene; standing at the front of the show, near the band, signified particularly strong allegiance, while occupying the back of the venue signified a lesser form of participation. Generally, as fans age they move from the front to the back of the room and, eventually, *out* of the room. Fonorow's work makes intuitive sense; ageing bodies create both physical limitations and symbolic boundaries around subcultural participation. Presumably, ageing traceurs will find leaping across rooftops increasingly difficult, b-boys will be sorer after dancing, and skaters will attempt fewer extreme tricks. Ageing rock fans limit their alcohol use and tone down their dancing, as their stamina declines and post-gig recovery time grows (Gibson 2012). Some goths tone down their macabre, androgynous, style; goth men found it harder "to 'get away with' feminine clothes or makeup once bodies had become larger, faces coarser, body hair denser and, in some cases, head hair sparser" (Hodkinson 2012: 141).

Still, ageing bodies do not automatically coincide with declining participation, even in the examples above. Studying the hardcore punk scene, Tsitos found that "older" (over 25) participants moshed or slamdanced less than they had in their youth, due both to "concerns over age-related physical limitations" and to "their disillusionment with perceived negative changes in the scene (reflected in increased violence in the pit)" (Tsitos 2012: 68). However, at times they *did* return to the pit, as moshing became a ritual by which to reconnect with friends, an effervescent moment of collective solidarity, emotional connection, and even physical intimacy. Ageing b-boys might feel more aches and pains, but given their years of experience they often mentor younger dancers, as "authority is often attributed to the ageing body, even after the peak performance years have passed" (Fogerty 2012: 55).

While many ageing subculturists tone down their spectacular styles and scene participation, some find ongoing meaning and even resistance in ostentatious stylistic displays. Given the connection between ageing bodies and social expectations, subculturists who continue (or begin) participating into adulthood upend dominant understandings of age-appropriate behavior, challenging the (restrictive) meanings of age. A tattoo-collecting 70-year-old defies conventional expectations of "old age." Studying a queer scene in Brisbane, Australia, Jodie Taylor (2012a) found that many post-youth participants continue partying, using drugs, and wearing more flamboyant fashions than their younger counterparts. Rather than change their participation to match their age, they alter "their perceptions of adulthood to ensure their continuing participation" (Taylor 2012a: 33). Ageing suggests a linear, heteronormative path – by a certain age, one should be married, purchasing a home, having and raising children, working a steady job, and eventually looking towards retirement. Prohibited, in most places, from marrying and forming conventional families, queer people disrupt the age timeline, as Judith Halberstam (cited in Taylor 2012a: 28) suggests: the "stretched-out adolescence" of "queer culture makers" disrupts "conventional accounts of subculture, youth culture, adulthood, and maturity." Likewise, Taylor's queer subjects resist *homo*normative ageing, particularly the premium that many queer scenes place upon youth and youthful *bodies*. In scenes where anyone over 30 is considered "old," ageing LGBTQs might find themselves judged by their peers as "tired old queens" or "bitter old dykes." Continued participation in supposedly youthful activities is personally gratifying and also an act of resistance. Queer subculturists (and many other subculturists as well) challenge the "successful/ unsuccessful" ageing dichotomy, thereby "queering" adulthood. Similarly, adult "alternative women" – sporting, for example, extensive tattoos, piercings, and crazy hair – disrupt the hyperfeminine "model woman" portrayed in the media (Holland 2004).

HOW DO OLDER AND YOUNGER SCENESTERS GET ALONG?

Even as many subculturists age and post-youth subcultural identification increases, in many scenes much of the energy and consistent participation remains with youth. How do such youth perceive their elders? Some youth see older, less active scenesters as sell-outs, as somehow less authentic (see Chapter 5). Likewise, scene elders may doubt youths' authenticity as they construct an idealized past, remembering things as better, more real "back in the day" as a way to bolster their own scene credibility (see Peterson 1997). These **jaded scenesters** lament the changes in, and perceived decline of, the scene (Haenfler 2006). Older hobos sometimes see their younger counterparts as disrupting their nostalgic recreation of the past, while the younger train-riders see themselves as more authentic as they are *currently* taking risks riding the rails (Lennon 2007).

In other scenes, participants perceive generational differences as mere differences rather than arguing about authenticity related to age and ageing participation, with youth even venerating their older subcultural heroes (Bennett 2006). Age brings some subculturists legendary status as they find adult success while living by their own (subcultural) code (Davis 2006). For example, Keith Morris of hardcore bands Black Flag, Circle Jerks, and Off! still tours the world, wearing dreadlocks to his waist and screaming vocals to a multigenerational audience. And at age 55, skateboarding legend Tony Alva still skates, runs his own skate shops, and plays in a punk band. As I mentioned above in the context of riot grrrls and b-boys, these elders can serve as **subcultural mentors**, role models guiding new generations of participants as they pass on subcultural capital. Older graffiti writers often "apprentice" younger artists, teaching them both technique and subcultural values

(Docuyanan 2000). Some older b-boys regard younger participants in their crews as their sons, forming multigenerational extended families (Fogerty 2012). An ageing body might even lead some b-boys to "retire," but retirement was not the same as quitting. Retired b-boys might compete less, focusing less on improvement, but still dance, as well as increasing their time spent teaching and judging competitive events. Somewhat ironically, as adult subculturists' participation *decreases*, their subcultural capital can *increase*.

Many scenes remain dominated by youth, going through ongoing generational turnover even as a small number of older participants remains active. However, **continuing scenes** feature a consistently active cohort that ages together within the scene (Smith 2009). For example, the average age of participants at the Whitby Gothic Weekend, a gothic festival held since 1994 in the UK has increased substantially in its nearly 20 years (Hodkinson 2012). Old acquaintances reconnect, talk about careers and families, and party, although perhaps not so vigorously as they had in their youth. Many bring their young children to the festival, often dressed in child-sized gothic attire (Hodkinson 2013b). Rather than ageing out of the scene, this ageing cohort changed its very nature, making the festival more family-friendly as organizers adapted the festival to accommodate parents with children. Festivals and reunion shows become portable or **temporary communities**, periodically bringing together diverse groups for relatively short spans of time (Gardner 2004). As subculturists who came of age since the subcultural explosion of the late 1970s/early 1980s – punk, skateboarding, metal, hip hop, graffiti-writing, and so on – grow older, it is possible we may witness more continuing scenes.

SUBCULTURAL CAREERS: HOW DO "OLDER" SUBCULTURISTS BLEND PARTICIPATION WITH MORE "CONVENTIONAL" RESPONSIBILITIES?

Born in Aberdeen, South Dakota in 1930, Fakir Musafar, father of the "modern primitive" movement and legendary figure in the body modification, fetish, and kink scenes, continues to tour, write, and film into his eighties. He earned degrees in electrical engineering and creative writing, served in the Army, and ran his own advertising agency. After practicing piercing and other forms of body play in relative secret for many years, Fakir "came out" at a tattoo convention in 1979 and has since made body play his career. His subcultural career, begun in his youth, became his livelihood later in life. Once a deviant outsider, Fakir now lectures at universities and passes on his skills to students in his San Francisco piercing school. And he is far from the only subculturist to incorporate his passions into "conventional" life. Early influential skateboarders such as Stacey Peralta and Tony Hawk, now in their forties and fifties, have not only started their own skateboard companies but have branched into filmmaking, video game production, and philanthropy. They have children, homes, and many of the trappings of "normalcy." Now in his fifties, David Ellefson of world-renowned metal band Megadeth, a band sometimes criticized for its violent imagery, has beaten his drug and alcohol addictions and returned to his Lutheran religious roots, starting his own ministry and studying at seminary (DeSantis 2012). These lives exemplify the circuitous life course of many subculturists who, while perhaps not so famous, blend their subcultural identities and behaviors with other pursuits. Rather than casting subcultural participation in opposition to conventional life (which has little meaning anyway), much better to observe exactly *how* subculturists age, what they *do*, and how they *make sense* of what they do.

Recall from Chapters 1 and 7 that scenes are fluid and porous rather than stable and fixed. Likewise, the boundaries of "youth" shift and change; one does not step over some imaginary line and magically, irrevocably, become an adult, as the number of adults who enjoy comic books, video games, toy collecting, and other "childish" pursuits can attest. Rather, young people in their twenties, especially in developed countries, see themselves as slowly progressing toward adulthood as they explore a variety of identities and possibilities for their futures. **Emerging adulthood** describes the period from late-teens to mid-twenties when young people have significant independence from their parents but have not yet committed to marriage, children, home ownership, or a lasting career (Arnett 2000). Many young people, including many subculturists, do not see these transitions as clear markers of adulthood, emphasizing instead taking personal responsibility for one's life.

So adulthood is ambiguous, and as we have seen many subculturists do not make a "clean break" from their respective scenes. Rather, we can think of subculturists' involvement as part of a **deviant career** (Becker 1963), in some ways paralleling the stages of conventional careers. However, deviant careers differ from conventional careers in significant ways. Where conventional careers are typically linear paths of increasing status, stability, and compensation, deviant (and subcultural) careers tend to be less linear, with people exiting and entering lifestyles (Best and Luckenbill 1982; see also Adler and Adler 1983). Subcultural careers may peak relatively early while offering little or no financial compensation, as in the case of graffiti-writers.

GRAFFITI-WRITING CAREER

Nancy Macdonald's (2001) study of New York and London graffiti subcultures reveals that many writers follow a similar progression through their deviant careers:

- Noticing graffiti: wherein a potential writer discovers graffiti and learns it can confer a sort of "fame."
- Tagging/bombing: a new writer chooses a graffiti name ("tag"), develops a style, and illegally tags her moniker in public places.
- Making a name: the writer's fame grows the more she tags.
- Throw ups: the writer progresses from simple signature tags to more larger, more complicated depictions of their tag.
- Piece promotion: in which the writer graduates to even larger, more mural-like designs often utilizing images in addition to stylized letters.
- Career decline: reputation established, many older participants' write less often. Legal penalties increase, financial and family responsibilities take on greater importance.
- Retirement or going legit: Some writers "retire" their names and fully enter into conventional roles. Others go legit by painting only in legal spaces, doing mural commissions, or turning their skills into full-time work as designers or other professional artists.

SUBCULTURAL WORK

Subcultures may appear to be (and in some part *are*) escapist retreats in stark contrast with conventional work. They seem to foster leisure and play, while work suggests responsibility, punctuality, and perhaps even drudgery. The classic film *Quadrophenia* depicts mods feeling truly free only when hanging out with their mates, just as *Saturday Night Fever* portrays the disco scene as a fun refuge from the protagonist's boring, oppressive work life. Yet the work/play dichotomy in which work is mundane and boring and leisure fulfilling and liberating is misleading (see Haenfler 2012b). Sometimes people enjoy their jobs; the bike messengers I discussed in Chapter 7 transform their work into play (Kidder 2011). Others, like some hardcore MMORPG gamers, turn their leisure into work, grinding through repetitive tasks in what should be enchanting virtual worlds (Rowlands 2012).

Subcultural experiences translate into careers in several ways (Haenfler 2011). **Scene careerists** such as professional musicians, promoters, record label owners, and artists create full-time employment related to a subculture. Professional musicians may be the most obvious example, but others include pro skateboarders, parkour fitness trainers, and mechanics who customize cars or motorcycles. Most of the older punks Tsitos (2012) studied maintained their connection to the scene by running record labels, playing in bands, or booking shows. **Hybrid scenesters** combine conventional and subcultural work (for pay), or sometimes blend the two, as in the case of Brazilian graffiti artist Nunca, whose work is found both on the streets and in art galleries. **Semi-retired subculturists** have even less connection to a scene, yet still somehow bring their subcultural values to bear on their work. Danielle Konya, a tattooed vegan straight edge desert chef, uses her Vegan Treats bakery not only to produce delicious food but also to promote cruelty-free living. Her business very consciously and openly advocates for animal rights, actively supporting a variety of animal advocacy organizations (Konya n.d.). Konya's example shows that some subculturists infuse their subcultural practices into even seemingly "conventional" careers.

Parents often worry that their child's subcultural involvement will negatively impact the kid's future: subcultural involvement is a waste of time better spent focusing on academics or more productive, resumé-building extracurricular activities. Perhaps of even greater concerns for parents are that the more permanent, bodily transformations – namely, tattoos and piercings – associated with many subcultures might be off-putting to future employers. While it is certainly the case that subculturists often face stigma in conventional settings (see Chapter 6), subcultural identities and bodily symbols can actually be *assets* in some careers. Tattoos, piercings, subcultural knowledge, and scene networks may advance careers in tattooing, fashion, music, and small businesses such as boutiques catering to subculturists (Driver 2011b). Hackers and gamers may go on to work in computer science, drawing upon skills they learned in the amateur hacking scene. Riot grrrls grew into "riot women" and used their DIY skills to organize feminist music festivals such as Ladyfest (Schilt and Zobl 2008). Someone with neck tattoos and stretched ears may have trouble landing a job at a major law firm. That same person looking to start an online "alternative" jewelry business might have an advantage, might carry a certain cache or authenticity in the eyes of potential customers. Subcultural *skills*, *identities*, *networks*, and even *bodies* serve as **subcultural career capital** in may jobs. In an era in which traditional manufacturing and even white collar jobs contract, the ability to create one's own job, even a DIY career, might be increasingly relevant.

Finally, subcultures resonate in unexpected ways even as older participants have little or no connection to their scene of origin. The "maker" subculture applies the DIY ethic to technological innovation, bringing together an array of people of all ages who love tinkering, building, experimenting, and learning. Participants make everything from robots and laser harps to aerial surveillance planes and cigar box guitars, often publishing (free) online guides detailing their work. They gather in online forums and also at Maker Faires. Some adherents come directly from other sorts of subcultures, but many do not. Still, the roots of the maker movement draw upon punk, open source, and hacker subcultures. As an example, in 1988, prominent maker Mark Frauenfelder cofounded "The World's Greatest Neurozine," *bOING bOING*, now an established blog with paid employees. His career, launched by a *print 'zine*, has since included being an editor at *Wired* magazine, authoring several books, and editing *MAKE* magazine. Makers' entrepreneurial spirit has caught the attention of venture capitalists, with *The Economist* (2011) magazine suggesting "The 'maker' movement could change how science is taught and boost innovation. It may even herald a new industrial revolution." Sounds similar to the hobbyist hacker culture of the 1970s that spawned Apple and Microsoft ...

PARENTING

In his book *Punk Rock Dad: No Rules, Just Real Life*, former Pennywise singer Jim Lindberg (2007: xxi) describes the balance between parenting three girls and screaming the lyrics to the punk band's anthem, "Fuck Authority," writing:

> The whole alternative/punk movement can be seen as one childlike refusal to grow up and take on responsibility, and the image of the immature, tattooed, and pierced alternative slacker/stoner, addicted to Internet Porn and video games, has become the archetype that defines our entire generation. For me, becoming a parent became the one thing that finally forced me to grow up and accept that I wasn't a kid anymore.

Such comments betray a sense of intractable tension between parenthood and subcultural identity, children "forcing" their irresponsible parents to grow up. Indeed, the tension between being a good father and constantly being away from home on tour prompted Lindberg to leave the band. (He rejoined in 2012.) Yet Lindberg *does* manage "punk rock parenthood," explaining he still wears band t-shirts, he still skates and plays music, and his daughters listen to *his* music in the car. Perhaps more importantly, Lindberg emphasizes the punk rock *values* he hopes to pass to the next generation, even as the more mundane aspects of parenting threaten to quash his punk ideals:

> If instead of forcing our religions, dogmas, and short-sighted way of thinking on them, we could encourage them to think for themselves, and show them how to be gracious and tolerant, rather than selfish and close-minded, maybe we could in fact make the world a better place, simply by being good parents. Wasn't this supposed to be the underlying goal of punk music in the first place, that we were to expose society for the sham it was, in the dim hopes of replacing it with a better one?
>
> (Lindberg 2007: 193)

Past scholars made much of the "**generation gap**," emphasizing the vast differences – in values, tastes, language, and practices – between adults and youth of the 1950s, 60s, and 70s. Popular musicians and youthful subculturists reinforce this gap, claiming that the older generation has sold out, or, in the words of rap duo DJ Jazzy Jeff and the Fresh Prince, that "Parents Just Don't Understand." More recently, others suggest the gap may be narrowing, as the distance between generations' attitudes and interests closes. Andy Bennett (2008) finds that classic rock bands – Pink Floyd, Led Zeppelin, AC/DC – continue to appeal to younger generations, taking on almost mythical significance as the original, most authentic expression of rock music. Such music becomes part of a "heritage discourse of rock" that "enshrines particular rock musicians of the late 1960s and early 1970s not merely as sub- or countercultural icons, but as key contributors to the essential character of late late-twentieth-century culture" (Bennett 2008: 266). Similarly, young metalheads continue to almost universally revere Black Sabbath as the originators of "heavy" music, despite being born long after the band's original demise. Many youth discover such music listening with their parents or thumbing through parents' vinyl record collections. DVDs, music television channels, and YouTube make watching classic performances easy, providing younger participants a time capsule in which to perpetually explore. Thus punk, hip hop, skateboarding, goth, and other subcultures are increasingly intergenerational.

Joe Kotarba (2002: 119) found that baby boomer rock 'n' roll fans shared both their musical tastes and values as they became parents and grandparents, with rock music serving as a "bridge across the generations" despite the common perception that music is a source of intergenerational tension. Mothers and daughters attend certain concerts together, fathers teach sons to play guitar. Certainly parents and their kids will argue about music, curfews, and clothing choices. But many parents also facilitate subcultural identities and scene involvement by purchasing concert tickets, taking kids to gigs, and, even if grudgingly, allowing their children to experiment with subcultural identities. The 1960s and 70s British Northern Soul scene, united by a love for obscure American soul music, has ebbed and flowed for several generations, peaking in the 1970s but persisting to today (Smith 2009, 2012). Early generations of "Soulies" teach their kids to dance, play soul music, and share their record collections with their children. Subcultural capital becomes a "family heirloom" *and* a scene that might otherwise have died off is given (thus far) perpetual life. Given that youth–parent "cultures" are not necessarily opposed, it makes sense to think of subcultures not only in terms of *youth resistance* but also in terms of **adult influence**. Parents with subcultural backgrounds can pass on subcultural capital (e.g. record collections, knowledge of scene histories) to their children – who may or may not be appreciative!

Subculturist parents, like any parents, pass on a certain set of values. These values may at times contradict their own subcultural experiences (Do as I say, not as I do!), but may also reflect subcultural politics. Thus a riot grrrl mother might take extra measures to encourage her daughter to be heard and to be a "cultural producer" rather than only a consumer (Schilt and Giffort 2012). They are also many times modeling to their kids a different approach to adulthood.

MOVING ON: WHAT ARE SUBCULTURES' RESIDUAL IMPACTS?

While some subculturists willfully choose to remain "outsiders" throughout their lives, others eventually shed most or all of their subcultural identities. (And there is some evidence that *women* decrease their participation more than men as women still take on a disproportionate share of childcare (Gregory 2009; Holland 2004).) Moving on does not, however, mean that subcultural participation has no lasting impacts. In fact, subcultural involvement often leaves strong **residual effects**, beliefs and behaviors nurtured in subcultural settings that transcend direct involvement in a scene. Studying ex-straight edgers, Jason Torkelson (2010) shows that despite abandoning abstinence and their edge identities former straight edgers claim the scene provoked lifelong changes, including spiritual seeking and activist identities such as animal rights and veganism (see also Wood 2007). Many became disillusioned with the movement's shortcomings, questioning its authenticity and its occasional militancy. Yet they also report that straight edge encouraged significant philosophical shifts lasting long into adulthood.

Older subculturists are not "inappropriately" hanging on to youth; they are "growing up" without forgetting their roots, often creatively reconciling adult responsibilities with scene identities (Hodkinson 2013a). The appeal of subcultural community, of living in some capacity at society's margins, transcends youth. As early participants in the "spectacular" subcultures of the 70, 80s, and 90s establish careers and become parents and grandparents, subcultural meanings change and boundaries shift. In fact, subcultures are part of a larger redefinition of youth and adulthood, providing adherents the space to question what it means to "grow up."

KEY INSIGHTS

- While popular media and even scholars portray subcultures as exclusively the domain of youth, adults *do* participate, even as many pursue careers and form families. Structural changes – in the economy, education, and gender roles – make possible the extension of "youth."
- *Subcultural* identities can resonate across the lifecourse, even as *scene* participation ebbs and flows. Older subculturists tend to focus less on style and consistent scene participation and more on the internalized values, lifestyles, and practices cultivated in the scene.
- Contrarily, many subculturists *do* continue their participation, periodically using style as a strategy and subcultural identity as a form of resistance to age-appropriateness.
- Subcultural careers are similar to conventional careers in many respects. However, while in conventional careers one's status tends to increase over time, subcultural careers are far less linear, with participants exiting and re-engaging over their lifecourse.

EXPLORING FURTHER

Ageing and Youth Cultures: Music, Style and Identity, edited by Andy Bennett and Paul Hodkinson, 2012 (Berg). The first edited collection of studies examining older subculturists' experiences, including sections on style, the body, and community.

Music, Style, and Aging: Growing Old Disgracefully? by Andy Bennett, 2013 (Temple University Press). Explores how varieties of music, from house to punk, as well as subcultural styles, continue to have personal and political significance to aging fans.

Rock On: Women, Ageing, and Popular Music, edited by Ros Jennings and Abigail Gardner, 2012 (Ashgate). A collection focused on the ways women, both performers and fans, negotiate ageing in relation to popular music.

"Spectacular Youth Cultures and Ageing: Beyond Refusing to Grow Up," by Paul Hodkinson, 2013 (*Sociology Compass* 7(1): 13–22). A brief article highlighting some of the key issues around subcultures and ageing.

Alternative Femininities: Body, Age and Identity, by Samantha Holland, 2004 (Berg). A study of women who intentionally resist cultural norms of femininity and ageing via body modifications and alternative styles.

The Other F Word, directed by Andrea Blaugrund Nevins, 2011. A documentary exploring the joys and contradictions surrounding punk rock fatherhood, including interviews with members of Pennywise, Blink 182, Rise Against, Red Hot Chili Peppers, Bad Religion, NOFX, and other bands.

Anvil: The Story of Anvil, directed by Sacha Gervasi, 2008. A funny and moving documentary following ageing Canadian metal band Anvil as they continue to pursue their passion 30 years after fading into obscurity.

BIBLIOGRAPHY

Acland, C. R. (2000) "Fresh Contacts: Global Culture and the Concept of a Generation." In N. Campbell (ed.) *American Youth Cultures*. New York: Routledge, pp.31–52.

Adler, P. and P. Adler (1983) "Shifts and Oscillations in Deviant Careers: The Case of Upper-Level Drug Dealers and Smugglers." *Social Problems* 31(2): 195–207.

—— (2012) "The Control Society: Crisis Creation and The Death of Moderation." *Psychology Today* blog January 12, 2012. www.psychology today.com/blog/the-deviance-society/201201/the-control-society (accessed March 14, 2012).

Adorno, T. (1991) *The Culture Industry: Selected Essays on Mass Culture*, ed. J. M. Bernstein. London: Routledge.

Advertiser, The (1991) "Suicide Boy Obsessed by Heavy Metal." May 3, 1991. (Accessed online via Lexus/Nexus February 19, 2013).

AFP Newswire (2010) "Saudi 'Emo' Girls Busted by Religious Cops." May 23, 2010. www.abc.net.au/news/2010-05-23/saudi-emo-girls-busted-by-religious-cops/836866 (accessed March 13, 2012).

Altheide, D. (2002) *Creating Fear: News and the Construction of Crisis*. New York: Aldine De Gruyter.

—— (2006) *Terrorism and the Politics of Fear*. Lanham, MD: AltaMira Press.

Amos, H. (2012) "Russian Punk Band Were Doing Devil's Work, Says Leader of Orthodox Church." *Guardian*, March 24, 2012. www.guardian.co.uk/world/2012/mar/25/pussy-riot-devils-work-kirill (accessed April 2, 2012).

Anderson, N. (1923) *The Hobo: The Sociology of the Homeless Man*. Chicago: University Of Chicago Press.

Anderson, T. (2009) *Rave Culture: The Alteration and Decline of a Philadelphia Music Scene*. Philadelphia, PA: Temple University Press.

Andes, L. (1998) "Growing Up Punk: Meaning and Commitment Careers in a Contemporary Youth Subculture." In J. S. Epstein (ed.) *Youth Culture: Identity in a Postmodern World*. Malden, MA: Blackwell Publishers, pp. 212–231.

Arnett, J. J. (1996) *Metalheads: Heavy Metal Music and Adolescent Alienation*. Boulder, CO: Westview Press.

—— (2000) "Emerging Adulthood: A Theory of Development From the Late Teens Through the Twenties." *American Psychologist* 55(5): 469–480.

Associated Press (2012) "Anders Behring Breivik Trained for Mass Killing with Video Games *Call of Duty*, *World of Warcraft*." *Daily News*, April 19, 2012. www.nydailynews.com/news/world/anders-behring-breivik-wanted-bomb-royal-palace-article-1.1064074 (accessed April 23, 2012).

Attwood, F. (2007) "Sluts and Riot Grrrls: Female Identity and Sexual Agency." *Journal of Gender Studies* 16(3): 233–247.

Avelar, I. (2011) "Otherwise National: Locality and Power in the Art of Sepultura." In J. Wallach, H. M. Berger, and P. D. Greene (eds) *Metal Rules the Globe: Heavy Metal Music Around the World*. Durham, NC: Duke University Press.

Azerrad, M. (2001) *Our Band Could Be Your Life: Scenes from the American Indie Underground 1981–1991*. New York: Little, Brown and Company.

Bailey, B. (2005) "Emo Music and Youth Culture." In S. Steinberg, P. Parmar and B. Richard (eds) *Encyclopedia of Contemporary Youth Culture*. Westport, CT: Greenwood Press.

Banchs, E. (2013) "Desert Sounds – Kalahari Metalheads Pursue a Dream." *Guardian*, February 10, 2013. www.guardian.co.uk/world/2013/feb/10/kalahari-metalheads (accessed February 11, 2013).

Barnett, E. (2012) "Rebels With a Cause: Bostwana's Heavy Metal Heads." *CNN*, July 4, 2012. www.cnn.com/2012/06/29/world/africa/botswana-heavy-metal-heads (accessed February 11, 2013).

Bartholomew, R. E. and E. Goode (2000) "Mass Delusions and Hysterias: Highlights from the Past Millennium." *Committee for Skeptical Inquiry* 24(3).

Baudrillard, J. (1995) *Simulacra and Simulation*, trans. S. F. Glase. Ann Arbor, MI: University of Michigan Press.

Bauman, Z. (1998) *Globalization: The Human Consequences*. Cambridge, UK: Polity Press.

—— (2000) *Liquid Modernity*. Cambridge, UK, and Malden, MA: Polity.

—— (2011) *Collateral Damage: Social Inequalities in a Global Age*. Cambridge, MA: Polity.

BBC News (2005) "French MP Blames Riots on Rappers" BBC News, November 24, 2005. http://news.bbc.co.uk/2/hi/europe/4467068.stm (accessed March 14, 2012).

Beal, B. (1996) "Alternative Masculinity and its Effects On Gender Relations in the Subculture of Skateboarding." *Journal of Sport Behavior* 19(3): 204–220.

Beck, U. and E. Beck-Gernsheim (2002) *Individualization: Institutionalized Individualism and its Social and Political Consequences.* Thousand Oaks, CA: Sage.

Becker, H. (1963) *Outsiders: Studies in the Sociology of Deviance.* New York: Free Press.

—— (2004) "Jazz Places." In A. Bennett and R. A. Peterson (eds) *Music Scenes: Local, Translocal, and Virtual.* Nashville: Vanderbilt University Press, pp. 17–27.

Beilharz, P. (2000) *The Bauman Reader.* Malden, MA: Wiley-Blackwell.

Bennett, A. (1999) "Subcultures or Neo-Tribes? Rethinking the Relationship Between Youth, Style, and Musical Taste." *Sociology* 33(3): 599–617.

—— (2005) "In Defence of Neo-Tribes: A Response to Blackman and Hesmondhalgh." *Journal of Youth Studies* 8(2): 255–259.

—— (2006) "'Punks Not Dead': The Significance of Punk Rock for an Older Generation of Fans." *Sociology* 40(1): 219–235.

—— (2008) "Things They Do Look Awful Cool: Ageing Rock Icons and Contemporary Youth Audiences." *Leisure* 32(2): 259–278.

—— (2013) *Music, Style, and Aging: Growing Old Disgracefully?* Philadelphia, PA: Temple University Press.

Bennett, A. and R. A. Peterson (eds) (2004) *Music Scenes: Local, Translocal, and Virtual.* Nashville: Vanderbilt University Press.

Bennett, A. and B. Robards (2012) "Editorial." *Continuum: Journal of Media & Cultural Studies* 26(3): 339–341.

Bessant, J. (1995) "'Hanging Around the Street': Australian Rockers, Sharpies, and Skinheads of the 1960s and Early 1970s." *Journal of Australian Studies* 19 (45): 15–31.

Best, A. (2006) *Fast Cars, Cool Rides: The Accelerating World of Youth and Their Cars.* New York: New York University Press.

Best, J. and D. F. Luckenbill (1982) *Organizing Deviance.* Englewood Cliffs, NJ: Prentice-Hall.

Bikini Kill (1993) "Resist Psychic Death." (song) *Yeah Yeah Yeah Yeah.* Kill Rock Stars.

Birrell, I. (2011) "Iceland Brought in from the Cold Thanks to Party of Punks and Pop Stars." *The Observer*, June 18, 2011, www.guardian.co.uk/world/2011/jun/19/iceland-reykjavik-mayor-best-party (accessed July 23, 2012).

Blackman, S. (2005) "Youth Subcultural Theory: A Critical Engagement with the Concept, its Origins and Politics, from the Chicago School to Postmodernism." *Journal of Youth Studies*, 8(1): 1–20.

Blazak, R. (2001) "White Boys to Terrorist Men: Target Recruitment of Nazi Skinheads." *American Behavioral Scientist* 44(6): 982–1000.

Bonilla-Silva, E. (2009) *Racism Without Racists: Color-Blind Racism and the Persistence of Racial Inequality in America* (3rd edition). New York: Rowman & Littlefield Publishers.

Bortree, D. (2005) "Presentation of Self on the Web: An Ethnographic Study of Teenage Girls' Weblogs." *Education, Communication, and Information* 5(1): 25–39.

Bourdieu, P. (1984) *Distinction: A Social Critique of the Judgment of Taste*, trans. R. Nice. Cambridge, MA: Harvard University Press.

Brake, M. (1985) *Comparative Youth Culture: The Sociology of Youth Culture and Youth Subculture in America, Britain, and Canada*. London: Routledge and Keegan Paul.

Braxton, A. (n.d.) "Brazilian Racial Formations – a Nation of Many Colors, Racial Classification in Brazil, Brazil: A Racial Paradise?" http://encyclopedia. jrank.org/articles/pages/6027/Brazilian-Racial-Formations.html (accessed January 6, 2013).

Breines, W. (1989) *Community Organization in the New Left, 1962–1968: The Great Refusal* (reissue edition). Piscataway, NJ: Rutgers University Press.

Brill, D. (2007) "Gender, Status and Subcultural Capital in the Goth Scene." In P. Hodkinson and W. Deicke (eds) *Youth Cultures: Scenes, Subcultures and Tribes*. New York: Routledge, pp. 111–125.

—— (2008) *Goth Culture: Gender, Sexuality, and Style*. Oxford: Berg.

Burghart, D. (ed.) (1999) *Soundtracks to the White Revolution: White Supremacist Assaults on Youth Music Subcultures*. Chicago: Center for a New Community.

Bury, R. (2005) *Cyberspaces of Their Own: An Ethnographic Investigation of Fandoms and Femininities*. New York: Peter Lang Publishers.

Cavan, R. S. (1983) "The Chicago School of Sociology, 1918–1933." *Urban Life* 11: 407–420.

Chambliss, W. (1973) "Foreword to 'The Saints and the Roughnecks'." http://alpha.fdu.edu/~peabody/Lexicon/Chambliss,_The_Saints_and_the_Roughnecks.html (accessed February 10, 2012).

Chaney, D. (2004) "Fragmented Culture and Subcultures." in A. Bennett and K. Kahn-Harris (eds) *After Subculture: Critical Studies in Contemporary Youth Culture*. Basingstoke, UK: Palgrave, pp. 36–48.

Chappell, B. (2012) *Lowrider Space: Aesthetics and Politics of Mexican American Custom Cars*. Austin, TX: University of Texas Press.

Chen, X., A. M. Orum, and K. E. Paulsen (2013) *Introduction to Cities: How Place and Space Shape Human Experience*. West Sussex, UK: Wiley-Blackwell.

Clark, D. (2004) "Waker Cells and Subcultural Resistance." *Peace Review* 16 (4): 453–457.

Clarke, J. (1976) "Style." In S. Hall and T. Jefferson (eds) *Resistance Through Rituals*. London: Routledge, pp. 175–191.

Clarke, M. (1974) "On the Concept of 'Subculture'." *The British Journal of Sociology* 25(4): 428–441.

Cohan, M. (2012) "The Problem of Gears and Goggles: Managing Membership Boundaries and Identities in the Steampunk Subculture." Presented at the Annual Meeting of the Pacific Sociological Association, San Diego, CA, March 22–25.

Cohen, A. (1955) *Delinquent Boys*. New York: The Free Press.

Cohen, S. (2002 [1972]) *Folk Devils and Moral Panics: The Creation of the Mods and the Rockers*. London: Routledge.

Condry, I. (2006) *Hip Hop in Japan: Rap and the Paths of Cultural Globalization*. Durham, NC: Duke University Press.

Corte, U. and B. Edwards (2008) "White Power Music and the Mobilization of Racist Social Movements." *Music & Arts in Action* 1(1).

Cowan, D. E. and D. G. Bromley (2007) *Cults and New Religions: A Brief History*. Malden, MA: Wiley-Blackwell.

Craig, T. J. (2003) *Global Goes Local: Popular Culture in Asia*. Honolulu, HI: University of Hawaii Press.

Cressey, P. (1932) *The Taxi-Dance Hall: A Sociological Study in Commercialized Recreation and City Life*. Chicago: University of Chicago Press.

Critcher, C. (2003) *Critical Readings: Moral Panics and the Media*. Berkshire, England: Open University Press.

Davis, J. (2006) "Growing Up Punk: Negotiating Aging Identity in a Local Music Scene." *Symbolic Interaction* 29(1): 63–69.

DeChaine, D. R. (1997) "Mapping Subversion: Queercore Music's Playful Discourse of Resistance." *Popular Music and Society* 21(4): 7–37.

Dedman, B. (2000) "Deadly Lessons: School Shooters Tell Why." Special report by the *Chicago Sun-Times*, October 15–16, 2000. http://powerreporting. com/files/shoot.pdf (accessed March 12, 2012).

Deegan, M. J. (1988) *Jane Addams and the Men of the Chicago School, 1892–1918*. New Brunswick, NJ: Transaction Books.

Delamere, F. M. and S. M. Shaw (2008) "'They See it as a Guy's Game': The Politics of Gender in Digital Games." *Leisure* 32(2): 279–302.

DeSantis, N. (2012) "Between Gigs, Megadeth Rocker Studies Online for the Lutheran Ministry." *The Chronicle of Higher Education*, February 26, 2012. http://chronicle.com/article/article-content/130938 (accessed February 20, 2013).

Dessier, M. (2006) "The Real Deal: Experiencing Authenticity in the Music of R. L. Burnside." MA thesis, Department of Sociology and Anthropology, University of Mississippi.

Diehl, M. (2007) *My So-Called Punk: Green Day, Fall Out Boy, The Distillers, Bad Religion – How Neo-Punk Stage-Dived into the Mainstream*. New York: St. Martin's Griffin.

Docuyanan, F. (2000) "Governing Graffiti in Contested Urban Spaces." *PoLAR: Political and Legal Anthropology Review* 1: 103–121.

Driver, C. (2011a) "Embodying Hardcore: Rethinking Subcultural Authenticities." *Journal of Youth Studies* 14(8): 975–990.

—— (2011b) "Hardcore Bodies in the Labour Market: On Subcultural Capital and Careers." Paper presented at the annual meetings of The Australian Sociological Association, November 2011, Newcastle, Australia.

Dunn, S. and S. McFadyen (directors) (2008) *Global Metal: 7 Countries, 3 Continents, 1 Tribe.* Film.

Du Plessis, M. and K. Chapman (1997) "Queercore: The Distinct Identities of Subculture." *College Literature* 24(1): 45–58.

Dyson, M. E. (2006) *Is Bill Cosby Right? Or Has the Black Middle Class Lost Its Mind?* New York: Basic Civitas Books.

Eckes, A. and T. Zeiler (2003) *Globalization and the American Century.* New York: Cambridge University Press.

Economist, The (2011) "More Than Just Digital Quilting." December 3, 2011. www.economist.com/node/21540392 (accessed December 5, 2012).

Elder, M. (2012) "Feminist Punk Band Pussy Riot Take Revolt to the Kremlin." *Guardian*, February 2, 2012. www.guardian.co.uk/world/2012/feb/02/pussy-riot-protest-russia?intcmp=239 (accessed April 2, 2012).

—— (2012) "Pussy Riot Sentenced to Two Years in Prison Colony for Hooliganism." *Guardian*, August 17, 2012.www.guardian.co.uk/music/2012/aug/17/pussy-riot-sentenced-two-years (accessed October 29, 2012).

Embrick, D. G., J. T. Wright, and A. Lukacs (eds) (2012) *Social Exclusion, Power and Video Game Play: New Research in Digital Media and Technology.* New York: Lexington Books.

Eyerman, R. and A. Jamison (1998) *Music and Social Movements: Mobilizing Traditions in the Twentieth Century.* Cambridge: Cambridge University Press.

Feagin, J. (2010) *The White Racial Frame: Centuries of Racial Framing and Counter-Framing.* New York and London: Routledge.

Federal Bureau of Investigation (2011) "2011 National Gang Threat Assessment – Emerging Trends." www.fbi.gov/stats-services/publications/2011-national-gang-threat-assessment (accessed March 12, 2012).

Feldman, C. J. (2009) *We Are the Mods: A Transnational History of a Youth Subculture.* New York: Peter Lang.

Fine, G. A. (1979) "Small Groups and Culture Creation: The Idioculture of Little League Baseball Teams." *American Sociological Review*, 44(5): 733–745.

Fine, G. A. and S. Kleinman (1979) "Rethinking Subculture: An Interactionist Analysis." *American Journal of Sociology* 85(1): 1–20.

Flintoff, C. (2012) "In Russia, Punk-Rock Riot Girls Rage Against Putin." NPR, February 8, 2012. www.npr.org/2012/02/08/146581790/in-russia-punk-rock-riot-girls-rage-against-putin (accessed April 2, 2012).

Fogerty, M. (2012) "'Each One Teach One': B-boying and Ageing." In P. Hodkinson and A. Bennett (eds) *Ageing and Youth Cultures: Music, Style, and Identity*. London and New York: Berg, pp. 53–65.

Fonorow, W. (1997) "The Spatial Organization of the Indie Music Gig." In K. Gelder and S. Thornton (eds) *The Subcultures Reader*. London and New York: Routledge, pp. 360–372.

—— (2006) *Empire of Dirt: The Aesthetics and Rituals of British Indie Music*. Middletown, CT: Wesleyan University Press.

Force, W. R. (2009) "Consumption Styles and the Fluid Complexity of Punk Authenticity." *Symbolic Interaction* 32(4): 289–309.

Forman, M. (2002) *The Hood Comes First: Race, Space, and Place in Rap and Hip Hop*. Hanover, New Hampshire: Wesleyan University Press.

Fox, K. J. (1987) "Real Punks and Pretenders: The Social Organization of a Counterculture." *Journal of Contemporary Ethnography* 16(3): 344–370.

Fraley, T. (2009) "I Got a Natural Skill ... Hip-Hop, Authenticity, and Whiteness." *The Howard Journal of Communications* 20: 37–54.

Frank, T. (1998) *The Conquest of Cool: Business Culture, Counterculture, and the Rise of Hip Consumerism*. Chicago, IL: University of Chicago Press.

Frazier, E. F. (1939) *The Negro Family in the United States*. Chicago: University of Chicago Press.

Friedman, G. (1981) *The Political Philosophy of the Frankfurt School*. Ithaca, NY: Cornell University Press.

Frith, S. (1978). *The Sociology of Rock*. London: Constable.

Frosdick, S. and P. Marsh (2005) *Football Hooliganism*. Devon, UK: Willan Publishing.

Frost, L. (2001) *Young Women and the Body: A Feminist Sociology*. New York: Palgrave.

Furlong, A. (2012) *Youth Studies: An Introduction*. New York and London: Routledge.

Furness, Z. (2010) *One Less Car: Bicycling and the Politics of Automobility*. Philadelphia, PA: Temple University Press.

Gardner, R. O. (2004) "The Portable Community: Mobility and Modernization in Bluegrass Festival Life." *Symbolic Interaction* 27(2): 155–178.

Gergen, K. (2000) *The Saturated Self: Dilemmas of Identity in Contemporary Life*. New York: Basic Books.

Gibson, L. (2012) "Rock Fans' Experiences of the Ageing Body: Becoming More 'Civilized'." In P. Hodkinson and A. Bennett (eds) *Ageing and Youth Cultures: Music, Style, and Identity*. London and New York: Berg, pp. 79–91.

Giddens, A. (1991a) *The Consequences of Modernity*. Palo Alto, CA: Stanford University Press.

—— (1991b) *Modernity and Self-Identity*. Palo Alto, CA: Stanford University Press.

Gieryn, T. F. (2000) "A Space for Place in Sociology." *Annual Review of Sociology* 26: 463–496.

Giffort, D. (2012) "The 'Slightly Sweeter' Riot Grrrl: Subculture, Commodification, and Reappropriation at Rock Camp." Paper presented at the 14th annual Chicago Ethnography Conference, April 2012, Chicago, IL.

Glassner, B. (2010) *The Culture of Fear: Why Americans Are Afraid of the Wrong Things*. New York: Basic Books.

Goddyer, I. (2003) "Rock Against Racism: Multiculturalism and Political Mobilization, 1976-81." *Immigrants & Minorities* 22(1): 44–62.

Goffman, E. (1963) *Stigma: Notes on the Management of a Spoiled Identity*. New York: Simon & Shuster.

Goode, E. and N. Ben-Yahuda (1994) *Moral Panics: The Social Construction of Deviance*. Malden, MA: Blackwell Publishers.

—— (2009) *Moral Panics: The Social Construction of Deviance* (2nd edition). Malden, MA: Blackwell Publishers.

Goodwin, J. and J. M. Jasper (2009) *The Social Movements Reader: Cases and Concepts* (2nd edition). Malden, MA: Blackwell Publishers.

Gordon, M. M. (1947) "The Concept of the Sub-Culture and its Application." *Social Forces* 26(1): 40–42.

Gramsci, A. (1971) *Selections from the Prison Notebooks of Antonio Gramsci*, ed. and trans. G. Smith and Q. Hoare. New York: International Publishers Co.

Grazian, D. (2003) *Blue Chicago: The Search for Authenticity in Urban Blues Clubs*. Chicago: University of Chicago Press.

Greenberg, A. (2007) *Youth Subcultures: Exploring Underground America*. New York: Pearson-Longman.

Gregory, J. (2009) "Too Young to Drink, Too Old To Dance: The Influences of Age and Gender on (Non) Rave Participation." *Dancecult: Journal of Electronic Dance Music Culture* 1(1): 65–80.

—— (2012) "Ageing Rave Women's Post-Scene Narratives." In P. Hodkinson and A. Bennett (eds) *Ageing and Youth Cultures: Music, Style, and Identity*. London and New York: Berg, pp. 37–49.

Grillo, I. (2008) "Mexico's Emo-Bashing Problem." *Time*, March 27, 2008. www.time.com/time/arts/article/0,8599,1725839,00.html (accessed March 12, 2012).

Haenfler, R. (2004a) "Manhood in Contradiction: The Two Faces of Straight Edge." *Men and Masculinities* 7: 77–99.

—— (2004b) "Rethinking Subcultural Resistance: Core Values of the Straight Edge Movement." *Journal of Contemporary Ethnography* 33(1): 406–436.

—— (2006) *Straight Edge: Clean Living Youth, Hardcore Punk, and Social Change*: Piscataway, NJ: Rutgers University Press.

—— (2011) "Making a Living While Living Clean: Older Straight Edgers' Pathways into Work and Careers." Paper presented at the annual meeting of the Australian Sociological Association, November 2011. Newcastle, Australia.

—— (2012a) "'More Than the X's on My Hands': Older Straight Edgers and the Meaning of Style." In P. Hodkinson and A. Bennett (eds) *Ageing and Youth Cultures: Music, Style, and Identity*. London and New York: Berg, pp. 9–23.

—— (2012b) "Working at Play and Playing at Work." Book review essay. *Qualitative Sociology* 35: 469–472.

—— (2012c) *Goths, Gamers, and Grrrls: Deviance and Youth Subcultures*. New York and London: Oxford University Press.

—— (2013) "Countercultures." In D. A. Snow, D. Della Porta, B. Klandermans, and D. McAdam (eds) *The Wiley-Blackwell Encyclopedia of Social and Political Movements*. Malden, MA: Wiley-Blackwell.

—— (forthcoming) "Punk Goes Glocal." In A. Bennett and S. Waksman (eds) The *Handbook of Popular Music*. London: Sage.

Haenfler, R., B. Johnson, and E. Jones (2012) "Lifestyle Movements: Exploring the Intersection of Lifestyle and Social Movements." *Social Movement Studies* 11(1): 1–20.

Halberstam, J. (1998) *Female Masculinity*. Durham, NC: Duke University Press.

—— (2005) *In a Queer Time & Place: Transgender Bodies, Subcultural Lives*. New York: New York University Press.

Hall, S. (1973) "Encoding and Decoding in the Television Discourse." Birmingham, UK: Centre for Cultural Studies, University of Birmingham, pp. 507–517.

Hall, S. and T. Jefferson (eds) (1976) *Resistance Through Rituals: Youth Subcultures in Post-War Britain*. London: Hutchinson.

Hall, S., C. Critcher, T. Jefferson, J. Clarke, and B. Roberts (1978) *Policing the Crisis*. London: Macmillan.

Harkness, G. (2008) "Hip Hop Culture and America's Most Taboo Word." *Contexts* 7(3): 38–42.

Harper, D. (2006) *Good Company: A Tramp Life* (updated edition). Boulder, CO: Paradigm Publishers.

Harrison, A. K. (2008) "Racial Authenticity in Rap Music and Hip Hop." *Sociology Compass* 2(6): 1783–1800.

—— (2009) *Hip Hop Underground: The Integrity and Ethics of Racial Identification*. Philadelphia: Temple University Press.

Hasan, A. and N. Hasan (2011) "It's a Tale of Two Acehs for 2 Events." *Jakarta Globe*, December 12, 2011. www.thejakartaglobe.com/news/its-a-tale-of-two-acehs-for-2-events/484111 (accessed February 10, 2012).

Hasan, N. (2011) "Aceh 'Punks' Arrested for 'Re-education'." *Jakarta Globe*, December 13, 2011. www.thejakartaglobe.com/home/aceh-punks-arrested-for-re-education/484549 (accessed March 12, 2012).

Healey, K. (2005) "'Empowered Erotica'?: Objectification and Subjectivity in the Online Personal Journals of the Suicide Girls." MA Thesis, Department of Culture, Literature and Society, University of Canterbury.

Heath, J. and A. Potter (2004) *Nation of Rebels: Why Counterculture Became Consumer Culture.* New York: Harper Business.

Hebdige, D. (1979) *Subculture: The Meaning of Style.* London: Methuen.

Hills, M. (2002) *Fan Cultures.* New York and London: Routledge.

Hochhauser, S. (2011) "The Marketing of Anglo-Identity in the North American Hatecore Metal Industry." In J. Wallach, H. M. Berger, and P. D. Greene (eds) *Metal Rules the Globe: Heavy Metal Music Around the World.* Durham, NC: Duke University Press, pp. 161–179.

Hodkinson, P. (2002) *Goth: Identity, Style and Subculture.* Oxford: Berg.

—— (2012) "The Collective Ageing of a Goth Festival." In P. Hodkinson and A. Bennett (eds) *Ageing and Youth Cultures: Music, Style, and Identity.* London and New York: Berg, pp. 133–145.

—— (2013a) "Spectacular Youth Cultures and Ageing: Beyond Refusing to Grow Up." *Sociology Compass* 7(1): 13–22.

—— (2013b) "Family and Parenting in an Ageing 'Youth' Culture: A Collective Embrace of Dominant Adulthood?" *Sociology* doi: 10.1177/0038038512454351.

Holland, S. (2004) *Alternative Femininities: Body, Age and Identity,* Oxford: Berg.

Hollander, J. A. and R. L. Einwohner (2004) "Conceptualizing Resistance." *Sociological Forum* 19(4): 533–554.

Hollingworth, S. and K. Williams (2009) "Constructions of the Working-Class 'Other' Among Urban, White, Middle-Class Youth: 'Chavs', Subculture and the Valuing of Education." *Journal of Youth Studies* 12(5): 467–482.

Hopkinson, N. (2012) *Go-Go Live: The Musical Life and Death of a Chocolate City.* Durham, NC: Duke University Press.

Hopper, C. B. and J. Moore (1983) "Hell on Wheels: The Outlaw Motorcycle Gangs." *Journal of American Culture* 6(2): 58–64.

—— (1990) "Women in Outlaw Motorcycle Gangs," *Journal of Contemporary Ethnography* 18(4): 363–387.

Hutcherson, B. and R. Haenfler (2010) "Musical Genre as a Gendered Process: Authenticity in Extreme Metal." *Studies in Symbolic Interaction* 35: 101–131.

Jacques, A. (2001) "You Can Run But You Can't Hide: The Incorporation Of Riot Grrrl Into Mainstream Culture." *Canadian Women's Studies* 20(3): 46–51.

Jenkins, H. (2002) "The Chinese Columbine: How One Tragedy Ignited the Chinese Government's Simmering Fears of Youth Culture and the Internet." *MIT Technology Review,* August 2, 2002, www.technologyreview.com/Infotech/12913 (accessed August 23, 2012).

—— (2006) *Fans, Bloggers, and Gamers: Exploring Participatory Culture*. New York: New York University Press.

Jenkins, P. (1992) *Intimate Enemies: Moral Panics in Contemporary Great Britain*. New York: Aldine De Gruyter.

Jones, K. and D. Maas (directors) (2012) *Punk in Africa*. Film.

Jones, O. (2012) *Chavs: the Demonization of the Working Class*. London and New York: Verso.

Kaltefleiter, C. K. (2009) "Anarchy Girl Style Now: Riot Grrrl Practices and Action." In R. Amster, A. DeLeon, L. Fernandez, A. J. Nocella, II, and D. Shannon (eds) *Contemporary Anarchist Studies*. New York and London: Routledge.

Kearney, M. C. (2006) *Girls Make Media*. New York: Routledge.

Keeler, W. (2009) "What's Burmese about Burmese Rap?" *American Ethnologist* 36(1): 2–19.

Kelly, K. (2012) "When Black Metal's Anti-Religious Message Gets Turned on Islam." *The Atlantic*, July 12, 2012. www.theatlantic.com/entertainment/archive/2012/07/when-black-metals-anti-religious-message-gets-turned-on-islam/259680/# (accessed July 19, 2012).

Kennedy, H.W. (2005) "Illegitimate, Monstrous, and Out There: Female Quake Players and Inappropriate Pleasures." In J. Hallows and R. Mosley (eds) *Feminism in Popular Culture*. London: Berg, pp. 183–202.

Kenney, P. (2003) *A Carnival of Revolution: Central Europe 1989*. Princeton, NJ: Princeton University Press.

Kidder, J. L. (2006) "'It's the Job That I Love': Bike Messengers and Edgework." *Sociological Forum* 21(1): 31–54.

—— (2011) *Urban Flow: Bike Messengers and the City*. Ithaca, NY: Cornell University Press.

—— (2012) "Parkour, The Affective Appropriation of Urban Space, and the Real/Virtual Dialectic." *City & Community* 11(3).

Kimmel, M. (1996) *Manhood in America: A Cultural History*. New York and Oxford: Oxford University Press.

Kitwana, B. (2005) *Why White Kids Love Hip Hop: Wangstas, Wiggers, Wannabes, and the New Reality of Race in America*. New York: Basic Books.

Konya, D. (n.d.) "Bio" on the Vegan Treats website. www.vegantreats.com (accessed December 5, 2012).

Kosut, M. (2006) "An Ironic Fad: The Commodification and Consumption of Tattoos." *Journal of Popular Culture* 39(6): 1035–1048.

Kotarba, J. A. (2002) "Baby Boomer Rock 'n' Roll Fans and the Becoming of Self." In J. A. Kotarba and J. M. Johnson (eds) *Postmodern Existential Sociology*. Walnut Creek, CA: Alta Mira Press.

Kruse, H. (1993) "Subcultural Identity in Alternative Music Culture." *Popular Music* 121: 31–43.

Kuhn, G. (2010) *Sober Living for the Revolution: Hardcore Punk, Straight Edge, and Radical Politics.* Oakland, CA: PM Press.

La Fontaine, J. S. (1998) *Speak of the Devil: Tales of Satanic Abuse in Contemporary England.* Cambridge: Cambridge University Press.

Leblanc, L. (1999) *Pretty in Punk: Girls' Gender Resistance in a Boy's Subculture,* Piscataway, NJ: Rutgers University Press.

Lee, S. and R. Peterson (2004) "Internet-Based Virtual Music Scenes: The Case of P2 in Alt.Country Music." In A. Bennett and R. A. Peterson (eds) *Music Scenes: Local, Translocal, and Virtual.* Nashville: Vanderbilt University Press, pp. 187–204.

Lennon, J. (2007) "Too Dirty to be a Hobo?" In A. Greenberg (ed.) *Youth Subcultures: Exploring Underground America.* New York: Pearson Longman, pp. 212-223.

Leonard, M. (1997) "Paper Planes: Travelling the New Grrrl Geographies." In T. Skelton and G. Valentine (eds) *Cool Places: Geographies of Youth Cultures.* New York: Routledge, pp. 101–118.

Levine, M. (2008) *Heavy Metal Islam: Rock, Resistance, and the Struggle for the Soul of Islam.* New York: Three Rivers Press.

—— (2009) "Doing the Devil's Work: Heavy Metal and the Threat to Public Order in the Muslim World." *Social Compass* 56: 564–576.

Levy, A. (2006) *Female Chauvinist Pigs: Women and the Rise of Raunch Culture.* New York: Free Press.

Lewin, P. and J. P. Williams (2009) "The Ideology and Practice of Authenticity in Punk Subculture." In P. Vannini and J. P. Williams, *Authenticity in Culture, Self, and Society.* Burlington, VT: Ashgate, pp. 65–85.

Liew, K. K. and K. Fu (2006) "Conjuring the Tropical Spectres: Heavy Metal, Cultural Politics in Singapore and Malaysia." *Inter-Asia Cultural Studies* 7(1): 99–112.

Light, B., M. Griffiths, and S. Lincoln (2012) "'Connect and Create': Young People, YouTube and Graffiti Communities." *Continuum: Journal of Media & Cultural Studies* 26(3): 343–355.

Lindberg, J. (2007) *Punk Rock Dad: No Rules, Just Real Life.* New York: HarperCollins.

Lyng, S. (1990) "Edgework: A Social Psychological Analysis of Voluntary Risk-Taking." *American Journal of Sociology* 95(4): 876–921.

Macdonald, N. (2001) *The Graffiti Subculture: Youth, Masculinity, and Identity in London and New York.* New York: Palgrave Macmillan.

Maffesoli, M. (1996) *The Time of the Tribes: The Decline of Individualism in Mass Society,* trans. D. Smith. London: Sage.

Magnet, S. (2007) "Feminist Sexualities, Race and the Internet: An Investigation of Suicidegirls.com." *New Media & Society* 9(4): 577–602.

Marchart, O. (2004) "New Protest Formations and Racial Democracy." *Peace Review* 16(4): 415–420.

Massey, D. (1998) "Spatial Constructions of Youth Cultures." In T. Skelton and G. Valentine (eds) *Cool Places: Geographies of Youth Cultures*. London and New York: Routledge, pp. 121–129.

Mattson, K. (2001) "Did Punk Matter? Analyzing the Practices of a Youth Subculture During the 1980s." *Journal of American Studies* 42(1): 69–97.

Maxwell, I. (2003) *Phat Beats, Dope Rhymes: Hip Hop Down Under Comin' Upper*. Middletown, CT: Wesleyan University Press.

Mayer, A. P. (2011) "'Fist in the Face of God': The Decentralized Diffusion of Heavy Metal Music Through the Internet." MA thesis, Department of Sociology, University of Cincinnati. http://etd.ohiolink.edu/view.cgi?acc_num=ucin1314362557 (accessed March 6, 2013).

McAdam, D., S. Tarrow, and C. Tilly (2001) *Dynamics of Contention*. Cambridge: Cambridge University Press.

McGrane, S. (2010) "Icelander's Campaign is a Joke, Until He's Elected." *New York Times*, June 25, 2010. www.nytimes.com/2010/06/26/world/europe/26iceland.html (accessed July 23, 2012).

McKay, G. (1996) *Senseless Acts of Beauty: Cultures of Resistance*. New York: Verso.

McLeod, K. (1999) "Authenticity Within Hip-Hop and Other Cultures Threatened with Assimilation." *Journal of Communication* 49(4): 134–150.

McRobbie, A. (2000) *Feminism and Youth Culture*. London: Macmillan.

McRobbie, A. and J. Garber (1976) "Girls and Subcultures: An Explanation." In S. Hall and T. Jefferson (eds) *Resistance Through Rituals*. London: Routledge, pp. 209–222.

Mellucci, A. (1989) *Nomads of the Present: Social Movements and Individual Needs in Contemporary Society*. Philadelphia: Temple University Press.

Merton, R. (1938) "Social Structure and Anomie." *American Sociological Review* 3(5): 672–682.

Michaels, S. (2008) "Russia Declares War on Emo Kids." *Guardian*, July 21, 2008. www.guardian.co.uk/music/2008/jul/22/russian.emo (accessed March 13, 2012).

Michaels, S. and E. Johnson (2012) "Aceh's Fundamental Clash: Punk Meets Shariah Law." *Jakarta Globe*, February 26, 2012. www.thejakartaglobe.com/home/acehs-fundamental-clash-punk-meets-shariah-law/500313 (accessed March 12, 2012).

Miller, L. (2004) "Those Naughty Teenage Girls: Japanese Kogals, Slang, and Media Assessment." *Journal of Linguistic Anthropology* 14(2): 225–247.

Moore, J. B. (1993) *Skinheads Shaved for Battle: A Cultural History of American Skinheads*. Bowling Green, OH: Bowling Green State University Press.

Moore, R. (2005) "Alternative to What? Subcultural Capital and the Commercialization of a Music Scene." *Deviant Behavior* 26(3): 229–252.

—— (2010) *Sells Like Teen Spirit: Music, Youth Culture, and Social Crisis*. New York: New York University Press.

Moynihan, M and D. Søderlind (2003) *Lords of Chaos: The Bloody Rise of the Satanic Metal Underground*. Los Angeles, CA: Feral House.

Muggleton, D. (1997) "The Post-Subculturist." In S. Redhead (ed.) *The Clubcultures Reader: Readings in Popular Cultural Studies*. Oxford: Blackwell, pp. 185–203.

Muggleton, D. and R. Weinzierl (eds) (2003) *The Post-Subcultures Reader*. London: Berg.

Mullaney, J. L. (2007) "'Unity Admirable but Not Necessarily Heeded': Going Rates and Gender Boundaries in the Straight Edge Hardcore Music Scene." *Gender & Society* 21(3): 384–408.

—— (2012) "All In Time: Age and the Temporality of Authenticity in the Straight-Edge Music Scene." *Journal Of Contemporary Ethnography* 41(6): 611–635.

Nally, C. (2009) "Grrrly Hurly Burly: Neo-Burlesque and the Performance of Gender." *Textual Practice* 23(4): 621–643.

Nash, K. (2010) *Contemporary Political Sociology: Globalization, Politics, and Power* (2nd edition). Malden, MA: Wiley-Blackwell.

Novikova, L. (2011) "Khipstery: Novie Potrebitel'skie Strategii Molodezhi." In E. L. Omel'chenko and G. A. Sabirova (eds) *Novie Molodezhnie Dvizheniia i Solidamosti Rossii*. Ul'ianovsk: Ul'ianovsk State University Press, pp. 127–145.

Ntarangwi, M. (2009) *East African Hip Hop: Youth Culture and Globalization*. Champaign, IL: University of Illinois Press.

O'Connor, A. (2002) "Local Scenes and Dangerous Crossroads: Punk and Theories of Cultural Hybridity." *Popular Music* 21(2): 225–236.

—— (2003a) "Anarcho-Punk: Local Scenes and International Networks." *Journal of Anarchist Studies* 11(2): 111–121.

—— (2003b) "Punk Subculture in Mexico and the Anti-globalization Movement." *New Political Science* 25(1): 43–53.

—— (2004) "Punk and Globalization: Spain and Mexico." *International Journal of Cultural Studies* 7(2): 175–195.

—— (2008) *Punk Record Labels and the Struggle for Autonomy: The Emergence of DIY*. New York: Lexington Books.

Paris, J., and M. Ault (2004) "Subcultures and Political Resistance." *Peace Review* 16(4): 403–407.

Park, R. and E. W. Burgess (1922) *Introduction to the Science of Sociology*. Chicago: University of Chicago Press.

Peck, B. M., P. R. Ketchum, and D. G. Embrick (2011) "Racism and Sexism in the Gaming World: Reinforcing or Changing Stereotypes in Computer Games?" *Journal of Media and Communication Studies* 3(6): 212–220.

Peters, B. M. (2010) "Emo Gay Boys and Subculture: Postpunk Queer Youth and (Re)thinking Images of Masculinity." *Journal of LGBT Youth* 7 (2): 129–146.

Peterson, B. (2009) *Burning Fight: The Nineties Hardcore Revolution In Ethics, Politics, Spirit, And Sound*. Huntington Beach, CA: Revelation Books.

Peterson, L. (2008) "The New Yorker and Hipster Racism." *Racialicious* post July 14, 2008. www.racialicious.com/2008/07/14/the-new-yorker-and-hipster-racism (accessed August 14, 2012).

Peterson, R. A. (1997) *Creating Country Music: Fabricating Authenticity*. Chicago: University of Chicago Press.

—— (2005) "In Search of Authenticity." *Journal of Management Studies* 42(5): 1083–1098.

Piano, D. (2003) "Resisting Subjects: DIY Feminism and the Politics of Style in Subcultural Production." In D. Muggleton and R. Weinzierl (eds) *The Post-Subcultures Reader*. London: Berg, pp. 253–265.

Pilkington, H. (1994) *Russia's Youth and its Cultures: A Nation's Constructors and Constructed*. London and New York: Routledge.

Pilkington, H. and E. Omel'chenko (2013) "Regrounding Youth Cultural Theory in Post-Socialist Youth Cultural Practice." *Sociology Compass* 7(3): 208–224.

Polhemus, T. (1998) "In the Supermarket of Style." In S. Redhead, D. Wynne, and J. O'Connor (eds) *The Clubcultures Reader*. Oxford: Blackwell, pp. 148–151.

Portwood-Stacer, L. (2010) "Constructing Anarchist Sexuality: Queer Identity, Culture, and Politics in the Anarchist Movement." *Sexualities* 13(4): 479–493.

—— (2012) "Anti-Consumption as Tactical Resistance: Anarchists, Subculture, and Activist Strategy." *Journal of Consumer Culture* 12(1): 87–105.

Primm, E. (2004) *The American Bad-Ass: A Social History of the Biker*. PhD dissertation. Department of Sociology, University of Colorado.

Purchla, J. (2011) "The Powers That Be: Processes of Control in Crew Scene Hardcore." *Ethnography* 12(2): 198–223.

Reddington, H. (2007) *The Lost Women of Rock Music: Female Musicians of the Punk Era*. Aldershot, UK: Ashgate.

Redhead, S. (1990) *The End-of-the-Century Party: Youth and Pop Towards 2000*. Manchester, UK: Manchester University Press.

—— (1997) *The Clubcultures Reader: Readings in Popular Cultural Studies*. Oxford: Blackwell.

Refused (no date) "Refused Are Fucking Dead." www.burningheart.com/refused/refmanifest1.htm and www.burningheart.com/refused/refmanifest3.htm (accessed March 23, 2012).

Riley, S. C. E., C. Griffin, and Y. Morey (2010) "The Case for 'Everyday Politics': Evaluating Neo-Tribal Theory as a Way to Understand Alternative Forms of Political Participation, Using Electronic Dance Music Culture as an Example." *Sociology* 44: 345–363.

Roberts, M. and R. Moore (2009) "Peace Punks and Punks Against Racism: Resource Mobilization and Frame Construction in the Punk Movement." *Music and Arts in Action* 2(1): 21–36.

Robertson, R. (1995) "Glocalization: Time-Space, and Homogeneity-Heterogeneity." In M. Featherstone, S. M. Lash, and R. Robertson, *Global Modernities*. London: Sage.

Robinson, C. (2009) "'Nightscapes and Leisure Spaces': An Ethnographic Study of Young People's Use of Free Space." *Journal of Youth Studies* 12(5): 501–514.

Rohrer, F. (2007) "So Why Do 'Normal' People Get Tattoos?" *BBC News Magazine* http://news.bbc.co.uk/2/hi/7034500.stm (accessed March 19, 2012).

Ronald, J. (2012) "Alternative Performances of Race and Gender in Hip-hop Music: Nerdcore Counterculture." Master's Thesis. Department of Pan African Studies, University of Louisville.

Rowlands, T. (2012) *Video Game Worlds: Working at Play in the Culture of EverQuest*. Walnut Creek, CA: Left Coast Press.

Roznak, T. (1969/1995) *The Making of a Counterculture: Reflections on the Technocratic Society and Its Youthful Opposition*. Berkeley, CA: University of California Press.

Ruggero, E. (2012) "A City and Its Occupation: Occupy Philly, Punk Participation and the Importance of 'Context and Content' in Social Movement Studies." Paper presented at the 17th Conference on Alternative Futures and Popular Protest. Manchester Metropolitan University, Manchester, UK, April 1–3, 2012.

Rupp, L. and V. Taylor (2003) *Drag Queens at the 801 Cabaret*. Chicago: University of Chicago Press.

Sahagun, L. (1998) "The Twisted World of a 'Straight Edge' Gang." *LA Times*, January 29, 1998. http://articles.latimes.com/1998/jan/29/news/mn-13171 (accessed March 13, 2012).

Sandstrom, K. L., D. D. Martin, and G. A. Fine (2009) *Symbols, Selves, and Social Reality: A Symbolic Interactionist Approach to Social Psychology and Sociology*. New York and London: Oxford University Press.

Santrock, J. (2011) *Adolescence*, 14th edition. Columbus, OH: McGraw-Hill.

Savage, J. (2002) *England's Dreaming, Revised Edition: Anarchy, Sex Pistols, Punk Rock, and Beyond*. New York: St. Martin's Press.

Scheel, K. R. and J. S. Westefeld (1999) "Heavy Metal Music and Adolescent Suicidality: An Empirical Investigation." *Adolescence* 34(134): 253–273.

Schilt, K. (2003) "'A Little Too Ironic': The Appropriation and Packaging of Radical Feminism by the New Angry Women in Rock." *Popular Music and Society* 26: 5–19.

Schilt, K. and D. Giffort (2012) "'Strong Riot Women' and the Continuity of Feminist Subcultural Participation." In A. Bennett and P. Hodkinson (eds)

Ageing and Youth Cultures: Music, Style and Identity. London and New York: Berg, pp. 146–158.

Schilt, K. and E. Zobl (2008) "Connecting the Dots: Riot Grrrls, Ladyfests, and the International Grrrl Zine Network." In A. Harris (ed.) *Next Wave Cultures: Feminism, Subcultures, Activism.* New York and London: Routledge, pp. 171–192.

Schouten, J. W. and J. H. McAlexander (1993) "Market Impact of a Consumption Subculture: The Harley-Davidson Mystique." In W. F. Van Raaij and G. J. Bamossy (eds) *European Advances in Consumer Research* (Vol. 1). Provo, UT: Association for Consumer Research, pp. 389–393. (Accessed online www.acrwebsite.org/volumes/display.asp?id=11476, May 8, 2012.)

Schur, E. M. (1971) *Labeling Deviant Behavior: Its Sociological Implications.* New York: Harper and Row.

Seganti, F. R. and D. Smahel (2011) "Finding the Meaning of Emo in Youths' Online Social Networking: A Qualitative Study of Contemporary Italian Emo." *First Monday* 16(7). http://firstmonday.org/htbin/cgiwrap/bin/ojs/index.php/fm/article/view/3197/3021 (accessed May 21, 2012).

Shank, B. (1994) *Dissonant Identities: The Rock 'n' Roll Scene in Austin, Texas.* London: Wesleyan University Press.

Shaw, C. R. and H. D. McKay (1942) *Juvenile Delinquency in Urban Areas.* Chicago: University of Chicago Press.

Shildrick, T. and R. MacDonald (2006) "In Defense of Subculture: Young People, Leisure and Social Divisions." *Journal of Youth Studies* 9(2): 125–140.

Shildrick, T., S. Blackman, and R. MacDonald (2009) "Young People, Class, and Place." *Journal of Youth Studies* 12(8): 457–465.

Silver, D., T. N. Clark, and C. J. Navarro Yanez (2010) "Scenes: Social Context in an Age of Contingency." *Social Forces* 88(5): 2293–2324.

Skelton, T. and G. Valentine (eds) (1998) *Cool Places: Geographies of Youth Cultures.* London and New York: Routledge.

Smith, N. (2009) "Beyond the Master Narrative of Youth: Researching Ageing Popular Music Scenes." In D. B. Scott (ed.) *The Ashgate Research Companion to Popular Musicology.* Aldershot, UK: Ashgate.

—— (2012) "Parenthood and the Transfer of Capital in the Northern Soul Scene." In P. Hodkinson and A. Bennett (eds) *Ageing and Youth Cultures: Music, Style, and Identity.* London and New York: Berg, pp. 159–172.

Snow, D. A., Rochford, Jr., B., Worden, S. K. and Benford, R. D. (1986) "Frame Alignment Processes, Micromobilization, and Movement Participation." *American Sociological Review* 51: 464–481.

Sobel, M. E. (1981) *Lifestyle and Social Structure: Concepts, Definitions, Analyses.* New York: Academic Press.

Stiglitz, J. (2003) *Globalization and Its Discontents.* London: Norton.

Straw, W. (1991) "Systems of Articulation, Logics of Change: Communities and Scenes in Popular Music." *Cultural Studies* 5(3): 368–388.

Sutherland, E. H. and D. R. Cressey (1978) *Principles of Criminology* (10th edition). Philadelphia, PA: Lippencott.

Szemere, A. (2001) *Up from the Underground: The Culture of Rock Music in Post-Socialist Hungary*. University Park, Pennsylvania: Penn State Press.

Taylor, J. (2012a) "Performances of Post-Youth Sexual Identities in Queer Scenes." In P. Hodkinson and A. Bennett (eds) *Ageing and Youth Cultures: Music, Style, and Identity*. London and New York: Berg, pp. 24–36.

—— (2012b) *Playing It Queer: Popular Music, Identity and Queer World-Making*. Bern: Peter Lang.

Taylor, V. (1989) "Sources of Continuity in Social Movements: The Women's Movement in Abeyance." *American Sociological Review* 54: 761–775.

Thomas, W. I. and F. Znaniecki (1918–1920) *The Polish Peasant in Europe and America*. Chicago: University of Chicago Press.

Thompson, K. (1998) *Moral Panics*. London and New York: Routledge.

Thornton, S. (1995) *Clubcultures: Music, Media and Subcultural Capital*. Hanover, NH: Wesleyan University Press.

Thrasher, F. (1927) *The Gang: A Study of 1,313 Gangs in Chicago*. Chicago: University of Chicago Press.

Torkelson, J. (2010) "Life After (Straightedge) Subculture." *Qualitative Sociology* 33: 257–274.

Touraine, A. (1981) *The Voice and the Eye: An Analysis of Social Movements*. Cambridge: Cambridge University Press.

—— (2000) *Can We Live Together? Equality and Difference*. Palo Alto: Stanford University Press.

Tsitos, B. (2012) "Slamdancing, Ageing and Belonging." In P. Hodkinson and A. Bennett (eds) *Ageing and Youth Cultures: Music, Style, and Identity*. London and New York: Berg, pp. 66–78.

Tuan, Y. (2011 [1977]) *Space and Place: The Perspective of Experience*. Minneapolis: University of Minnesota Press.

Turkle, S. (1995) *Life on the Screen: Identity in the Age of the Internet*. New York: Touchstone.

—— (2011) *Alone Together: Why We Expect More from Technology and Less from Each Other*. New York: Basic Books.

Ulysses (2012) "Hip Hop and the Arab Uprisings." www.opendemocracy.net/ulysses/hip-hop-and-arab-uprisings (accessed May 25, 2012).

Vale, V. and A. Juno, eds. (1989) *Re/Search #12: Modern Primitives: An Investigation of Contemporary Adornment & Ritual*. San Francisco, CA: Re/Search Publications.

Valentine, G., T. Skelton, and D. Chambers (1998) "Cool Places: An Introduction to Youth and Youth Cultures." In *Cool Places: Geographies of*

Youth Cultures edited by T. Skelton and G. Valentine. London and New York: Routledge, pp. 1–32.

VanderMeer, J. (2011) *The Steampunk Bible: An Illustrated Guide to the World of Imaginary Airships, Corsets and Goggles, Mad Scientists, and Strange Literature.* New York: Abrams.

Van Meter, W. (2012) "Hip Hop's Queer Pioneers." *Details Magazine*, October 2012. www.details.com/celebrities-entertainment/music-and-books/201210/hip-hop-queer-pioneers (accessed February 6, 2013).

Vannini, P. and J. P. Williams (eds) (2009) *Authenticity in Culture, Self, and Society*. Burlington, VT: Ashgate.

Victor, J. S. (1993) *Satanic Panic: The Creation of a Contemporary Legend*. Chicago, IL: Open Court.

Walker, M. (1987) "Heavy Metal's Toll Among Russia's Young." *Guardian*, June 6, 1987.

Walker, R. (2003) "The Marketing of No Marketing." *New York Times*, 22 June 2003. www.nytimes.com/2003/06/22/magazine/the-marketing-of-no-marketing.html (accessed 3 May 2013).

Wallach, J. (2008) *Modern Noise, Fluid Genres: Popular Music in Indonesia, 1997-2001*. Madison, WI: Wisconsin University Press.

Washburne, C. J. and M. Derno (eds) (2004) *Bad Music: The Music We Love to Hate*. New York: Routledge.

Watkins, S. C. (2005) *Hip Hop Matters: Politics, Pop Culture, and the Struggle for the Soul of a Movement*. Boston, MA: Beacon Press.

West, C. (2001) *Race Matters*. Boston, MA: Beacon Press.

West, L. (2012) "The Complete Guide to Hipster Racism." *Jezebel* post, April 26, 2012. http://jezebel.com/5905291/a-complete-guide-to-hipster-racism (accessed August 14, 2012).

Whyte, W. F. (1955 [1943]) *Street Corner Society: The Social Structure of an Italian Slum*. Chicago: University of Chicago Press.

Widdicombe, S. and R. Wooffitt (1990) "'Being' Versus 'Doing' Punk: On Achieving Authenticity as a Member." *Journal of Language and Social Psychology* 9(4): 257–277.

—— (1995) *The Language of Youth Subcultures: Social Identity in Action*. Harlow, Essex: Harvester-Wheatsheaf.

Wilkins, A. (2004) "'So Full of Myself as a Chick': Goth Women, Sexual Independence, and Gender Egalitarianism." *Gender and Society* 18(3): 328–349.

—— (2005) "'It's an Aesthetic': Goth Freakiness and the Reproduction of White Middle Classness." Paper presented at the annual meeting of the American Sociological Association, Philadelphia, PA.

—— (2008) *Wannabes, Goths, and Christians: The Boundaries of Sex, Style, and Status*. Chicago, IL: University of Chicago Press.

Williams, D. J. (2008) "Contemporary Vampires and (Blood-Red) Leisure: Should We Be Afraid of the Dark?" *Leisure* 32(2): 513–539.

—— (2009) "Deviant Leisure: Rethinking 'The Good, The Bad, and the Ugly'." *Leisure Sciences* 31(2): 207–213.

Williams, J. P. (2009) "The Multidimensionality of Resistance in Youth-Subcultural Studies." *The Resistance Studies Magazine* 1: 20–33.

—— (2011) *Subcultural Theory: Traditions and Concepts*. Cambridge, UK, and Malden, MA: Polity.

Williams, J. P. and H. Copes (2005) "'How Edge Are You?' Constructing Authentic Identities and Subcultural Boundaries in a Straightedge Internet Forum." *Symbolic Interaction* 28(1): 67–89.

Williams, S. F. (2007) "'A Walking Open Wound': Emo Rock and the 'Crisis' of Masculinity in America." In Freya Jarman-Ivens (ed.) *Oh Boy!: Masculinities and Popular Music*. New York and London: Routledge, pp. 145–160.

Willis, P. (1977) *Learning to Labor: How Working Class Youth Get Working Class Jobs*. New York: Columbia University Press.

—— (1978) *Profane Culture*. London: Routledge and Kegan-Paul.

Willson, J. (2008) *The Happy Stripper: Pleasures and Politics of the New Burlesque*. London: I. B. Tauris & Co.

Wilson, A. (2007) *Northern Soul: Music, Drugs and Subcultural Identity*. Portland: Willan.

Wilson, B. (2002) "The Canadian Rave Scene and Five Theses on Youth Resistance," *Canadian Journal of Sociology* 27(3): 373–412.

Winge, T. (2008) "Undressing and Dressing Loli: A Search for the Identity of the Japanese Lolita." *Mechademia* 3: 47–63.

Wood, R. T. (2007) "A Straightedger's Journey." In A. Greenberg (ed.) *Youth Subcultures: Exploring Underground America*. New York: Pearson Longman, pp. 223–233.

Yinger, J. M. (1960) "Contraculture and Subculture." *American Sociological Review* 25: 625–635.

Yurchak, A. (1999) "Gagarin and the Rave Kids: Transforming Power, Identity and Aesthetics in Post-Soviet Nightlife." in A. M. Barker (ed.) *Consuming Russia: Popular Culture, Sex and Society Since Gorbachev*. Durham and London: Duke University Press, pp.76–109.

INDEX

Note: **bold** terms indicate key ideas bolded in the main text.

affective appropriation of space 120
age/ageing 90–1, 140–6, 149–150, 153–4; *see also* youth
anarchism 51–3, 57, 79
authenticity 33, 46, 67, 83–92, 97, 120, 142; and new media 125–6

Banksy 84–5
bedroom culture 71
bike messengers 92, 120
bikers 51, 63, 71, 95–6
Birmingham School 7–9, 32, 33, 66; contribution of 9; and **resistance** 45; and **style** 8–9
Black metal 113
blues music/musicians 87–88, 90, 119
b-boys 143–4, 146
body/bodies 77, 92–3; 149–150; and ageing 143–5; **body competency** 93
body modification 92, 146–7
bricolage 8
burlesque 72, 74
Burning Man 11

chavs 8, 63–4
Chicago School 3–5; contribution of 6–7; methods of 5; theory of deviance 4, 36;
Centre for Contemporary Cultural Studies (CCCS) *see* Birmingham School
clubculture theories *see* **post-subculture** studies
commercialization 93–9
consumption 12, 31, 46, 95
commodification *see* **consumption** and **commercialization**
cosplay 51
counterculture 20, 30
cultural capital 37; *see also* **subcultural capital**
cultural hegemony *see* **hegemony**
culture industry 94

deviance 4, 34, 102; theory of **social disorganization** 4, 36
defusion 97–8

deviant career 147–150
diffusion 97–8, 128–9, 132
DIY (Do It Yourself) 52, 54, 74, 99, 129, 150
Drag 79

edgework 38–39
electronic dance music (EDM) 11, 53
emo 49, 75, 79, 108, 113, 124

Fairey, Shepard 84–5
fan culture *see* **fandom**
fan fiction 73, 74
Fakir Musafar 18, 87, 146–7
fandom 22
femininity 47, 50, 72–5, 142, 145
folk devil 105
football hooligans 22, 120

gamers/gaming 74, 103, 125, 126–7, 149
gang 21
gender 70–6, 88, 127, 142; and resistance 73–6, 98–9
generation gap 151–2
globalization 127–130; and homogenization 130–2, resistance to 132–5
glocalization 130–1
go-go music 121–2
goth 50, 86, 143, 146
graffiti, graffiti-writing 32, 84–5, 120, 124–5; graffiti-writing career 148

hardcore *see* punk and straight edge
heavy metal 35, 68, 72, 88, 104; and globalization 131–2, 134; moral **entrepreneurial campaign** against 108–9
hegemonic masculinity *see* masculinity
hegemony 8, 44–45, 130
hip hop 33, 66–7, 71–2, 89, 120: and the Arab Uprisings 56; and **globalization** 131–2, 134;

moral **entrepreneurial campaign** against 114; nerdcore 75–6
hipster 31, 69, 85, 90, 94–5
hobos 140, 145
homology 9, 66
human ecology 4

identity 16, 55, 86; ascribed 29; virtual 126–7
idioculture 6
incorporation 98–9
individualization 29, 37

Juggalos 11, 36, 109

kogal culture 12, 74

labeling theory 6
leisure 7, 12, 19, 30, 38, 46; deviant leisure 34
lifestyle 19
lifestyle movement 52–3
Lolita culture 72–4
lowriders 65

mainstream 10, 15, 17, 37, 43; vs. underground 87, 91
maker culture 150
masculinity 50, 71, 75–6; female masculinity 79
modern primitives 18, 34
modernization 28–30
mods 132–3, 136
moral crusade *see* **moral entrepreneurial campaign**
moral entrepreneurial campaign 107–11, 135; **rule creators** and **enforcers** 109; *see also* **moral panic**
moral entrepreneur *see* **moral entrepreneurial campaign**
moral panic 9, 103–7; role of the media in 111–13; and video games 111
MTV 31, 128

neo-tribe 10–11, 46
new media 122–5; and **authenticity** 125–6
new religious movement 20–1
Northern Soul 38, 66, 152–3

Otaku 103, 109

Parent Music Resource Center (PMRC) 110
parenthood 146, 151–3
parkour 38, 93, 124–5
participatory culture *see* **fandom**
place 87, 119–121; **regulation** of 121
postmodernism 10, 31
post-subculture studies 10–13, 19, 38; contribution of 12–13; and **resistance** 45–7
prefigurative politics 52–53
privilege 44, 69, 74
psychological problems 34–5
punk 9, 42–3, 47, 54, 93; and **globalization** 132; and **moral panic** 111; and politics 57
Pussy Riot 42–3

queer 78–79, 144–5

race 52, 62, 64–70, 88–9, 97; **colorblind racism** 69–70, 89; **racial segregation** 65; whiteness 68–70, 89, 127
racism *see* **race** and **white racial frame**
rave 10, 38, 50, 120, 142
resistance 8, 17, 73–7; dimensions of 47–9; effectiveness of 50, 58, 98–9; and **globalization** 132–5; meanings, sites, and methods of 47–8; and music 55; political 42–3, 48, 52, 57–8
retrospective reinterpretation 115
riot grrrl 38, 43, 52, 74–5, 98–9, 129, 142
Rock Against Racism 54, 57
roller derby 72, 74

Sanguinarium *see* vampires
Satanic panic 105–6, 115; and black metal 113
scene 10–11; **continuing** scene 145; local, **translocal**, and **virtual** 121–3
self 29, 30, 39
sexual script 78
sexuality 72–3, 75, 76–9
sharpies 121–2
signification spiral 112
skateboarding 22, 24, 51, 76, 120, 147
skinhead 9, 32, 36
social class 7–8, 32, 45, 62–4, 89–90
social media *see* new media
social movement 19–20, 30, 43, 54–6
space *see* place
subcultural capital 37, 91–3, 134, 153
subcultural career *see* **deviant career**
subculture: definition and characteristics of 15–18, 25; emergence of 28–33; as **free spaces** and **abeyance structures** 54–5, 57; importance of studying 24–5; in Japan 49; and **innovation** 33; participation in 33–9; **scapegoating** of 114–16; as **strategy** 14, 39–40;
steampunk 12, 92, 122
stigma 6
stigma management *see* stigma
straight edge 47–8, 50, 55–6, 75–6, 126, 141–2, 153; and **moral panic** 112
strain theory 5–6, 35–7; and **status frustration** 36, 45
style 8–9, 45, 92–3; and ageing 141–2; **supermarket of** 10
suicide 35
Suicide Girls 76–7, 92

symbolic interactionism 14
tattoos 62, 90, 92, 128
traceurs *see* parkour

vampires, human 34

West Memphis Three 115
white power 55, 56, 57, 65–6
white racial frame 68–9; **counter-frame** 70

whiteness *see* race
women, and resistance 47, 72–3

youth 27, 30, 140–1, 147; **emerging adulthood** 147; and social contradictions 32

'zine 52, 55, 74, 129, 150